For Women
Who Grieve

For Women
Who Grieve

Embracing Life After the Death
of Your Partner

Tangea Tansley

THE CROSSING PRESS
FREEDOM, CALIFORNIA

Published in the U.S.A. by The Crossing Press in 1996

Copyright © 1995 by Tangea Tansley

First published in Australia in 1995 by Thomas C. Lothian Pty Ltd

Cover design by Victoria May

Cover photograph courtesy of Digital Stock Corp.

For information on bulk purchases or group discounts for this and other Crossing Press titles, please contact our Special Sales Manager at 800-777-1048.

Library of Congress Cataloging-in-Publication Data

Tansley, Tangea.
    For women who grieve: embracing life after the death of your partner/ Tangea Tansley.
        p.   cm.
    Originally published: Australia: Thomas C. Lothian, 1995.
    Includes bibliographical references and index.
    ISBN 0-89594-832-X (pbk.)
    1. Breavement--Psychological aspects. 2. Grief 3. Widows--Psychology
4. Widows--Life skills guides 5.Life change events.
I. Title
BF575.G7T36   1996
155.9'37'082--dc20   96-22340
                                                          CIP

Acknowledgments

....

My thanks to the people whose words and work I have quoted, and to my friend Athol Barrett for his unfailing help and support.

For permission to reprint, grateful acknowledgment is made to the following:

Quotation by Joseph Campbell, in Betty Sue Flowers (ed.), *The Power of Myth*. Copyright 1988 Apostrophe S Productions Inc. and Alfred van der Marck Editions.

Excerpt from Edgar Cayce, in Henry Reed, *Channeling Your Higher Self*. Copyright 1989 The Association for Research and Enlightenment Inc.

Quotation by Achaan Chah, in Jack Kornfield & Paul Breiter (comp. & eds), *A Still Forest Pool*. Copyright 1985 Jack Kornfield and Paul Breiter.

Quotation from C. G. Jung, in Aniela Jaffe (ed.), *C. G. Jung: Word and Image*. Copyright 1979 Princeton University Press; reprinted by permission.

Excerpt from Harriet Klein, 'The future precedes the past: Time in Toba,' vol. 38. Copyright 1978 Harriet Klein.

Reprint of Portia Nelson, *There's a Hole in My Sidewalk*, 'Autobiography in Five Short Chapters.' Copyright 1977 Portia Nelson.

Excerpt from Julian Boul Noies, *And the Walls Came Tumbling Down*. Copyright 1983 Julian Boul Noies.

Excerpt from M. Scott Peck, *The Road Less Travelled*. Copyright 1978 M. Scott Peck.

Excerpts from Pat Rodegast & Judith Stanton (eds), *Emmanuel's Book*. Copyright 1985 Pat Rodegast. Used by permission of Bantam Books, a division of Bantam Doubleday Dell Publishing Group Inc.

Siegfried Sassoon, *Collected Poems by Siegfried Sassoon*, 'Microcosmos.' Copyright 1947 Siegfried Sassoon and Faber & Faber.

Excerpts from Sogyal Rinpoche, *The Tibetan Way of Living and Dying*. Copyright 1992 Rigpa Fellowship.

Quotation by Thelma Thompson, quoting her father, in Dale Carnegie, *How to Stop Worrying and Start Living*. Copyright 1948 Dale Carnegie.

Excerpts from Stuart Wilde, *The Force*. Copyright 1974 Stuart Wilde.

Excerpts from Judith Wright, *Collected Poems 1942–1947*, 'Shadow.' Copyright 1971 Judith Wright. Reprinted with the permission of the publishers.

Every effort has been made to trace copyright owners. The publishers would be pleased to rectify any error or omission.

In memory of Austin …
To my wonderful family,
my friends, my dogs …
And Toni, who opened the door

Contents

....

Introduction

'Forward We March'

Men come and they go and they trot and they dance, and never a word about death. All well and good. Yet when death does come—to them, their wives, their children, their friends—catching them unawares and unprepared, then what storms of passion overwhelm them, what cries, what fury, what despair! ...

To begin depriving death of its greatest advantage over us, let us adopt a way clean contrary to that common one; let us deprive death of its strangeness, let us frequent it, let us get used to it; let us have nothing more often in mind than death. ...We do not know where death awaits us: so let us wait for it everywhere.

To practice death is to practice freedom. A man who has learned how to die has unlearned how to be a slave.

—*Michel de Montaigne*

The intensity of emotional turmoil I felt over the death of my husband went deep. I felt as if I were a piece of debris spinning at the edge of a cyclone. In my head, I was sure that if I could only make it to the center of the storm, the calm 'eye' of the cyclone, I would find the peace and stability I needed. Part of me knew that the world would gradually settle back on its axis and the memories that at that time brought such sharp darts of pain would one day become good memories, but my emotions were captive to a different beat.

I had been taken by surprise by death, and in the whirlwind of confusion that followed I lost my way. It was a new experience for me and I had no pattern to follow. There was no map to take me where I needed to go.

I spent many months alternating between panic and despair. My doctor spoke authoritatively about 'grieving properly.' I lacked a map for that, too. I believed I *was* grieving properly. So this is grief, I thought. Pain.

Pain is a part of life. As the psychologists tell us, it is difficult, and not desirable, to try to avoid it. In fact, in *The Road Less Traveled* psychotherapist M. Scott Peck maintains that suffering is essential for our mental health. In trying to sidestep pain, he says, 'the substitute itself ultimately becomes more painful than the legitimate suffering it was designed to avoid.' Peck's words echo those of others of his profession: pain is something we have to go through and not around. If we try to avoid it, it will only return more strongly at a later date.

So, given our interest in maintaining our sanity, pain is something that we have to accept and learn to live with. At the same time we do not have to wear it like a hair-shirt as I did. We do not have to lose our sense of direction, our sense of self. The pain can be understood and controlled and, in that way, lessened and made more palatable.

Whatever the depth of our love for and commitment to our mates, whatever we went through together, and however thorough we are about the process of 'grieving properly,' there is nothing written either in the stars above or down here on earth that insists that we have to put ourselves through torture. We only feel the intensity of the pain and confusion we do because we have been conditioned to treat death as a tragedy.

Talk of death and dying in our society is frequently taboo. People want to move the discussion to a 'more cheerful subject.' And when someone does die—whether the death is that of an elderly person, a friend in pain for whom death may be a welcome release or a canine companion well on in years—we react with gloom on hearing the news.

There is, however, no imperative for death to be a tragedy. We are free to view death, and react to it, as we wish. Everyone reacts differently. There are those women who have a built-in coping mechanism that allows them to accept the inevitable and move on. They are the lucky ones, and their numbers are few. There are others who are religious to differing degrees and who, through their religion, are able to accept the inevitable and come to terms with their grief. They, too, are lucky in that they know they are not alone, but part of a mighty circle of oneness. Another small group consists of people who have worked on themselves and their spirituality to the point where the information in this book will not be new, but already a part of their daily lives. They have worked hard to get out of the destructive path of the cyclone to the calm at the center. This book has not been written for these women; rather, it is written for women, like myself, who have been taken by surprise by death and who are perhaps not properly prepared for life. It is written for those who are not coping well or who would like to cope better. It is written as an experiential book, one that grew out of my own need, and will, I hope, meet the needs of those who stand where I stood at what seems just a moment ago.

While each loss carries its own particular set of difficulties, this book has been written specifically for women who, like me, have lost their mates. While men feel pain just as deeply as women, the sets of problems, fears and insecurities that face each sex are different, as are our physical and emotional needs and outlets. Also, as women we are statistically two-and-a-half times more likely than men to have to cope with the death of a mate. Men have a shorter life expectancy and die younger than women, whether from stress-related disease or accident. And since women have tended—although there is evidence that the trend is changing—to marry older men, the problem of women having to face life on their own, in many cases after several decades of companionship, is compounded.

If you are reading this book, you are probably feeling very sad. I can only say that we are all in this together, this life adventure. Your sadness is my sadness and the sadness of people everywhere who lose their loved ones. Like grief and pain, the sadness is not a bad thing. It just is. But together we can control the depth and duration of the sadness and work on it until, in its own time, it turns to joy. Joy that we were privileged to know our special men; joy for the care and love shown us by our children, our wider family and our friends; and joy reserved for the special day when the clouds dissolve and the color returns to the sky. Because, one day, it will.

In coping with my own grief, I drew great comfort from the writings and philosophies of others. Books I enjoyed and drew both wisdom and comfort from are mentioned in the text, and listed in the 'Further Reading' section at the end of this book.

It is important to understand a little about the grief process in order to monitor our progress through it. Understanding is the first step to greater pain control.

Grief usually follows three stages, which can be represented by three colors. After the shock of death has subsided, the first stage can manifest itself as rage or anger at the death of your loved one. This stage is also sometimes accompanied by guilt. And, not surprisingly, the color of this stage is red.

The second stage of the process is sorrow. We may be feeling sorry not only for our mates, but for ourselves too. This stage is often accompanied by depression or the deepening of stress. The color of this stage is black.

It is when we reach the third stage, that of letting go, that we are well on the way to recovery. The color of this stage is white, a symbol of our return to the light. Eastern religions conduct their funerals in white. White is the color of moving on. The purpose behind this book is to help you to reach the white as soon as possible.

Grief is inevitable, and it is necessary to pass through all three stages. That is what the doctors mean by 'grieving properly.' It is not only good, but healthy and absolutely essential for your complete recovery and continuing sanity. But to behave—as I did before I pieced together my own map—like a butterfly impaled through the abdomen is not healthy.

The book suggests a path you might follow on your way to recovery. There is a chapter on understanding why we feel the way we do about death, as well as chapters on getting out and about again, learning to meditate, the importance of interpreting your dream world, carrying on with the practicalities of life, and coping with your children's grief in addition to your own.

Each step along the path is designed to provoke your own thoughts and actions. My aim has been to suggest rather than convince, to shine a light on avenues you may not have known existed. The rest is up to you. The idea is not to escape pain, but to understand and move through it. If we learn how to handle grief, we can use it as a positive instead of a negative experience. We can learn to let it go in its own time, instead of clinging to it.

As my seventeen-year-old daughter wrote in one of her many uplifting notes to me after my husband's death, 'Forward we march.'

Chapter One

Understanding Death

Life and death
should not be considered as opposites.
It is closer to the truth
to speak of dying as an entrance
rather than an exit.

—*Emmanuel's Book*

$\large A$ large part of the pain we
experience over the death of a loved one comes about
because we do not understand death. To our modern,
linearly-conditioned minds, it comes at the end of a trail of
circumstances that started with our birth. We see birth at
the beginning of the trail, death somewhere in the distance,
in the future, at the end.

It seems we have forgotten, or perhaps we never learned,
that we are a part of nature and that nature is cyclical. The
planets rotate on their axes, the Earth revolves around the
sun, the seasons come and go, a seed germinates and grows
into a plant, which in turn flowers, sets seed and dies. The
seed of the flower is reborn as another tiny green plant, and
so the circle continues. Evidence of the cyclical world of
nature is all around us. But in the West we seem somehow
to separate ourselves from nature, almost refusing to
acknowledge that we, too, as living organisms, are part of
this cyclical process. Is it any wonder that death appears so

uncompromising and final, perceived as it is as lying somewhere in the future, along a road that ends in the murky
shadow of fate?

Since language to some extent mirrors thought processes,
the language of a region or culture can help to show how a
particular culture's concept of time is linked to its views on
life and death. In the English language, we can see how our
thought processes are expressed as metaphors clearly describing the way we perceive time. For English-speakers, the
future lies ahead, the past behind. We 'face' the future; we
meet it 'head on.' We trust our money troubles will disap-
pear 'down the road a piece.' We hope that the good times
lie 'ahead,' while we have put the bad times 'behind' us.

Our terms for expressing death work in a similar linear
way: our mate has 'passed on,' 'passed away,' 'gone to
heaven' or 'gone on ahead.' In other words, to the Western
way of thinking, as expressed by the English language, once
time—or life—has gone by, it has gone for good. Death represents finality. It's the wiggly line of the electrocardiogram
fading on the screen. Within the tightly woven arrogance of
our society, shaped by a conditioning condoned by our
ignorance, we rarely come into contact with other ways of
expression, other modes of thought. And, if we do, they're
held suspect or treated with scorn.

Other cultures express a different conception of time in
their individual languages, and, with it, a different approach
to life and death. In her paper, 'The future precedes the past:
Time in Toba,' Harriet Klein describes how the speakers of
the Toba language (natives of the Gran Chaco region of
South America) use primarily spatial terms in describing

time. Events are 'in view,' 'coming into view,' 'going out of view' or 'out of view.' Time is seen as circular with the distant past and distant future overlapping in the locational metaphor 'out of view.' In English the remote past and the remote future are, she says, 'totally different poles, whereas in Toba they can and do overlap.' For the Toba, the dead move into the west with the setting sun, going out of view and towards rebirth in the east. They see life and death as part of the same cyclical process.

The Balinese, through their ritual language of Kawi, see time as circular, following a series of concurrent tracks. Kawi has no metaphor to describe the passing of time, with the result that there is no view of time as a continuing stream of events. Take the Balinese calendar as an example. According to anthropologist Clifford Geertz,

> the cycles and supercycles [of the Balinese calendar] are endless, unanchored, uncountable, and, as their internal order has no significance, without climax. They do not accumulate, they do not build, and they are not consumed. They don't tell you what time it is; they tell you what kind of time it is.

Time in Bali has a sense of simultaneity, and events are the result of accidental co-occurrences. For the Balinese, the process of aging has no cultural significance; instead they place enormous value on the act of procreation.

In another example of language mirroring thought, the predominantly Buddhist inhabitants of Burma have organized the Burmese language into a system of concentric circles, with the Buddha's words, images and relics at the center, and other animate beings arranged according to their closeness to Buddha. Their language reflects their view of the world, which, again, is circular. Buddhists firmly believe in the cycle of death and rebirth, or *samsara*. This belief leads most Buddhists to a committed vegetarianism. To a Buddhist, a meat-eater is at risk of eating a relative or friend who has died.

There are countless other examples from the mass of different tribal societies and cultures that make up our world, but the picture is clear. The language of a culture provides us with a view of the thought processes expressed by that language. One of the reasons that other cultures do not treat death as the tragedy that we do in the West is because they do not think of death as coming at the end of a line. They do not view it as an event that is finished, closed, final, but rather as an opportunity for rebirth or renewal.

It is paradoxical that in the West, alongside our tendency to regard ourselves as more advanced than other cultures, we cope so comparatively poorly with death, something that should be regarded as a natural part of life. Perhaps our technocratic society has sucked the essence from our spiritual selves. If we regard ourselves as being apart from and above nature, superior to other animals, and with nothing to learn from other cultures, it is not surprising that we have come to see ourselves as invincible. Our conditioning and obeisance to the tangible materialism of our society only reinforces this view. Consequently, death *when* it comes (not if) is more of a shock than it should be.

We live at a time and in a society where life is increasingly seen as precious, where all our received messages are set to reinforce this idea, and where, if medical science had its way, we would never die. But that society is full of contradictions. It is considered a crime by some to cut off a life-support machine to allow a person to die in dignity, and a crime to abort a fetus resulting from rape. Sometimes, our society insists on life at any price, even when the price seems too high. And that on an already overcrowded planet.

No wonder things have gone wrong. We are so out of tune with nature that we are unable to look about us and perceive the simple cyclical truth that everything born must die. That is the only certain thing about life: one day we will die.

Instead of accepting this as a fact, we place death as far as possible from our minds, somewhere far in our linear future where it is distant enough to ignore. We continue to nourish the thought that we and our loved ones are invincible. Death is something that happens in films or to other people, but not to us. Not now. Not yet, anyway. And 'yet' is a long way off. We'll 'face' death and all it brings when the time comes.

Having pushed death into the far-off future, there is no point in 'spoiling' our current lives with sad thoughts. That's *how* we think. Pain is bad. Grief is bad. Sad is bad. And death is bad.

None of these things has to be bad. We do have the option of viewing them as part of the journey of life. No one, after all, was rash enough to promise us that life would be a joyride. It is composed of 'ups and downs,' happy and sad phases that balance each other out. The happy times are fairly easy to get through. We find the sad spells more difficult. But it is in these sad times, or times of pain, that we tend to experience the greatest growth. We cannot avoid pain. We have to go through it, for that is part of what it means to be a human being. At the same time, the pain need not cripple us. We do not have to stagger through the death of a loved one as human beings immobilized by grief. We can, but we don't *have* to.

Whether we regard the death of a mate as a tragedy, a cause for celebration, or somewhere in between, depends on our perception of death. And our perception of death is only a perception, shaped by the society in which we live. Death does not have to take place at the end of the road. It does not have to be final. It can be viewed as part of the cyclical process of life. It is all a question of attitude, and we can control our attitude. As Shakespeare wrote, 'There is nothing either good or bad, but thinking makes it so.' However, if we have never thought that way, it is not easy to shift decades of conditioning.

For me, it happened this way.

When my husband died I felt as though I had lost half my mind and half my body. I don't believe that any language has the words to describe a grief that for me was so appalling it went beyond emotional distress and became a physical pain that produced real terror. He was dead, and I had been left behind.

We'd had a pact, a sort of half-pact, that if he ever died I would too. That was the only time we ever discussed death, in a remote, totally impractical way. But I had the children. That was enough to make me stop long enough for reason to reassert itself. And something else: it was a long while before I realized he was really dead. He was a great jokester, and I quite expected him to pop out of the cupboard one day and say, 'Ha! Really had you worried that time!' I didn't want to risk playing Juliet to his Romeo.

Advice came from all sides. Out of my numbness I reacted like a puppet on an elastic string. The emphasis was always on time, on the road ahead. Some said, 'Time heals all wounds'; others, 'Time helps, but it never really heals'; and still others, 'It's something you never get over.' There were people who insisted, 'Keep busy,' and some who cautioned, 'Take time to reflect.' In my new awareness, I came across people who had been grieving for two years, five years, ten, twenty, and my panic grew. I wondered what to do. Was I to sit on the backs of my hands and wait to see how time decided to treat me? And how was I going to do that?

Into all this panic marched my sister with *Emmanuel's Book*. (Not the wink-wink, nudge-nudge Emmanuelle of the screen, but Emmanuel the kind and friendly spirit.) But not being particularly religious or spiritual-minded, I was in no hurry to read it, and *Emmanuel's Book* sat on the hall table for many days. However, one long evening, about four months after the death of my mate, I opened the book. That, for me, was the beginning of the healing process.

Once I started reading, a whole new world began to unfold. The physical and mental pain crystallized into an unsteady feeling that became something like a mix between learning to walk unaided and making an attempt at a new and unfamiliar language. It was not that the pain disappeared so much as that emotion akin to excitement began to dissipate the hopelessness. I gradually became aware that I was not alone, that the world I had been born into was both more complex and more beautiful than I had ever imagined. He hadn't 'gone on ahead and left me behind.' Although there was certainly nothing instantaneous about the change, I gradually became able to control my grief instead of allowing it to control me.

What I needed most in those early days was the reassurance that my husband had not deserted me. *Emmanuel's Book* gave me that reassurance. It allowed me to consider the fact that my mate could now be my spirit-husband. When he was alive hadn't we called each other soul mates? Well, now he could be a real soul mate, couldn't he? And if that were possible, wasn't it a good time to put it to the test? So, since both mornings and nights were particularly difficult times for me, instead of drowning in grief I started talking to him as I lay in bed. I told him of my problems, fears and loneliness. And just as in life he had soothed and encouraged me, so he did now. I no longer felt alone.

I would like to make it clear that I was not—and am not—becoming a spiritualist or a mystic, joining a religious secret society or dashing off to ouija sessions. Starting from a basis of skepticism and pragmatism, I was more concerned to start on a journey of investigation that would bring me as close to the truth as it was possible to get. To do this, it became necessary to allow that other cultures might have a more accurate view of life and death than my own, that alongside my material world a spiritual world may well exist, and that the concepts of life after death and reincarnation were real possibilities. I slowly began to realize that I was not alone, but part of a oneness that leads back to the source of life itself.

In a sort of arbitrary, unstructured fashion, I began to read everything I could find on the universe and its laws. I read across the spectrum, from the Bible, the Koran and the *Bhagavad Gita* to the works of poets, writers and philosophers.

I found that the first record of dualism—acknowledgment that we have both body and soul—was espoused by the Greek philosopher Plato four centuries before the birth of Christ. I was comforted by poet-philosopher Ralph Waldo Emerson's transcendentalism, by Walt Whitman's thought-provoking poetry, by Kahlil Gibran's gentle words of wisdom, by translations from the eighteenth-century Latin of the Swedish mystic Emanuel Swedenborg, and by the American mystic Edgar Cayce's readings on people's past lives.

Here were people whose philosophies and writings had survived the test of time. If they believed that there was more to life than our rather haphazard existence on this planet—which for me up until that time had been more of a coin toss than a spiritual journey—why should I not at least give some credence to their thoughts? I started to read more modern works. I discovered Stuart Wilde's books on the forces that exist within and around us, including his inspirational paperback *Life Wasn't Meant to Be a Struggle.* For Christmas the children gave me physicist Darryl Reanney's marvelous book on our flawed perception of time, *The Death of Forever*, in which he provides scientific evidence that the higher states of consciousness are 'timeless.' For the first time, there was scientific proof that our concept of time is but one concept. I began to attend New Age seminars, talks and shows.

All this combined to show me that there was a huge and convincing body of thought out there that maintained that it was just as likely that there was life after death as it was that life ends with the death of the body. Half the world believed one way, the other half the other. I was free to choose.

And so, based on my reading, study, observations and personal experiences, slowly my mindset changed. Where I had previously been convinced that my life on this planet was a one-time shot at achieving, at material success, I started to question my concept of 'success.' I had equated ambition with aiming for the top rung of the ladder. Now I started to wonder about that top rung: whether once there a person would be wiser or able to see farther or more clearly, or whether life then became a static thing. Just what exactly was that top rung? As I began to question, I started to see my time on Earth as a stopover, as one portion only of a journey that might, for all I knew, spread over several lifetimes. For part of one of those lifetimes, my mate and I had been privileged to share our earthly lives. There was more to come.

The idea of viewing life on Earth as a schoolroom, as a place where we learn our lessons and ideally gather wisdom for use in another life, made sense to me then, and it still does. It was a piece that had been missing from the jigsaw puzzle of my life. I came, gradually, to the realization that there is nothing bad, nothing to be feared, in death. I began to see that the treatment of death as a grand tragedy was a product of our Western civilization, a civilization that places importance on keeping people alive at any cost. I began to see things in perspective. And I have come full circle to the point at which I started this chapter.

It is not death itself that is bad. It is our understanding of death that is at fault. Death is simply part of a process that begins at birth. To dread the inevitable seems all wrong, a sad and useless overreaction to what is a natural part of life. To experience grief at your loss is natural and healthy; to wish yourself dead—as I did—is not.

In the ancient language of Pali in which the old Buddhist texts were written, birth and death were linked in the one word, *jati-marana*—birth-death. In many African, American Indian and Australian aboriginal tribes, death is viewed as going to another country, as just another stage in the journey. Some Eastern religions celebrate the death of relatives as the gateway to a better land. Funerals are conducted with drums and flowers, and the 'mourners' are revellers who dress in white. Even Asians who are Christians have a different view of death from ours. On a visit to Death Street in Singapore, you are more likely to see bottles of rice wine being popped at raucous all-night parties than any sign of trauma following the death of a relative. When I informed a Chinese friend of my husband's death, instead of providing the usual condolences, she took it in such a matter-of-fact way that at first I wondered whether she had heard what I had said. I was used to people feeding my feeling-sorry-for-myself feeling. Of all cultures in the Western world, it is probably the Irish who take the most pragmatic attitude, using the event of a death as an excuse for a spirited wake.

So it seems that only in our technocratic society is this birth-death connection, this *jati-marana*, broken. We greet birth with celebration, death with dread, when in fact both processes are part of the same journey.

But we do have a choice. We can change our attitude. We can reflect on Shakespeare's words 'There is nothing either good or bad. ...' We can learn to understand our grief—and allow that grief to be a healthy, natural part of missing a loved one's physical presence—instead of throwing up our hands and half-dying ourselves. Just as understanding leads to mastery over our bodies in childbirth, so in exactly the same way knowledge and understanding can help us through the process of grief.

Time *is* the great healer. There is no doubt about that. At the same time, there are many practical ways in which we can help time along. The first step in the healing process is to understand that we do have a choice about how we view death.

Chapter Two

Letting Go

Do everything with a mind that lets go. Do not expect any praise or reward. If you let go a little, you will have a little peace. If you let go a lot, you will have a lot of peace. If you let go completely, you will know complete peace and freedom. Your struggles with the world will have come to an end.

—*Achaan Chah*

The next stage in the recovery process is learning how to 'let go' of your grief at the right time. And the 'right time,' of course, varies with each person and set of surrounding circumstances. First, let us take a general look at the process of letting go, and then look for clues on timing.

Properly developed, the art of letting go can go beyond helping you to face today's problem and can be turned into an important life skill. Letting go means unlearning the habits of leaning, clinging and smothering, and allowing others their physical and mental space in the form of thoughts and opinions. Letting go means living *with* others, but not *for* others. It means planting your own garden, or working on your own self-esteem to achieve your potential without living your life through another person.

The Lebanese poet-philosopher Kahlil Gibran says it all in a line in *The Prophet* that is used often in marriage ceremonies: 'The oak tree and the cypress grow not in each other's shadow.' Once learned, the skill can be applied broadly across all areas of your life, or specifically to cope with a nagging problem that would benefit from being temporarily shelved, a love affair that has gone wrong, or the acknowledgment that it is time for a child to leave home.

You may be saying, 'What has all this to do with me? I was *forced* to let go. I need to know what to do *now*.' Well, another word for letting go is acceptance. To suggest you let go is just another way of saying, 'Accept.' Stop fighting circumstances beyond your control. Let go. Accept.

There is no better time in your life than *now* to start putting letting go, or acceptance, into practice. Because, like all skills, letting go does take practice and, believe me, there are a thousand different times each day it can be practiced! Help the mental discipline along by writing it on your bathroom mirror with soap or lipstick: 'Let go!' Learning to see and accept this big event in your life for what it is will help you from now on with a plethora of other circumstances. Instead of going into a spin when things don't quite go your way, try a mental shrug every now and then. Ask yourself just how important in the overall scheme of things it is that this particular circumstance go exactly as you planned it. Maybe it is important. Maybe it isn't. You can't tell until you examine it quietly.

And so, having started the mental exercise with these affirmations, it is time to get physical with the art of letting go. This can best—and soonest—be achieved by the natural acts of crying and laughing and talking.

To suggest that you should cry would seem to be unnecessary since, for some people, crying is the easy part. It is stopping the flow of tears that is difficult. But there are others who feel that they should not show their feelings, especially in public. How often do you hear the awed respect underlying the words 'She's being very brave about it all'?

If you want to cry, cry. We are not living out a dehumanized Orwellian fantasy. We are living in the real world where something has happened to us that we don't quite understand. We feel lost without our partner, and it's going to take us time to familiarize ourselves with the new rules and get ourselves out of the path of the cyclone. We want to get out of this storm the best way we can, as soon as we can. Crying is as good a place as any to start. Far from being applauded, putting on a 'brave face' is categorized as a repressive and antiquated custom by late-twentieth-century psychology.

It is essential to realize that crying is an important and natural part of the healing process, particularly for the female sex, for whom crying is acknowledged as a physiological necessity. It releases built-up tension and, while you may feel either better or worse directly afterwards, emotionally it will have a long-term cleansing effect. A bit of stormy crying and pillow-punching and railing at fate will usually leave you so exhausted that you will sleep, and wake up feeling better.

But some people cannot cry. It's not that they are too concerned about the stiff-upper-lip nonsense; they would cry if they could, but they can't. If you are one of those, go off on your own—preferably to a deserted beach or forest—and yell at the top of your voice for as long and hard as you can. You may not be able to cry, but you can certainly yell. Yell, shake your fists, allow yourself to get really mad, and stop just short of getting hoarse. If yelling makes you feel as self-conscious as crying, pull the plug on the tension by increasing your exercise quota. If you are a jogger, jog just a little bit harder. If you are a tennis player, pretend you're Martina Navratilova and really whack that ball around the court. If you swim, take on an extra lap or two. Exercise is one of the best antidotes available to depression and stress. If you are one of those people who can't cry and do not play sports, think seriously about what type of physical activity you can build into your current lifestyle. If you cook, pummel that dough or stir that polenta; if you garden, dig, chop or hoe; around the house, now's the time to scrub the floor and wash down the paintwork, or tackle spring cleaning. A friend of mine belongs to a choir and finds that nothing relieves stress more than a few sessions of 'primal screaming' in some dramatic choral work. Stop thinking about it and *do* it. If all else fails, you can always peel onions.

In other words, let off steam in any way that comes naturally to you. Whatever your faith or philosophy, you have had a shock and are not only allowed, but encouraged, to express your feelings. Let all the rage, unhappiness and loneliness—all the 'Why did it have to happen to me?'—pour out.

There will come a time when you will be brave enough to realize just *why* you are crying or feeling glum. You are not crying for your mate, you are crying for *you*. Your mate is okay right now. The chances are that he is more okay than you are at this moment. If he had been debilitated by a prolonged illness or disease, his suffering is now at an end. That surely is occasion for relief, celebration even, not grief. Or if he died suddenly and quickly, that too is something to be relieved about. You cannot grieve because someone you loved is no longer in pain or died *before* he suffered undue pain. Either way, for him death is a win-win situation, although it may not look that way to you at the present.

So be clear about the reason for your tears. Without criticizing or being hard on yourself, you should be aware of the true reason for your grief. Sooner or later there will come a stage in the healing process when you become aware that the only reason you are crying is because you are feeling sorry for yourself. And that is okay, too. Suddenly you have the children or the dogs or the cats, or perhaps all of them, to worry about. Singlehandedly, you think. And then there's the mortgage. Or getting a job. Or upgrading your skills to bring in more cash.

In short, there are pressures on you that weren't there before. And you don't feel up to handling any of it. So it is important to acknowledge this. If you want to feel sorry for yourself for a little while, the indulgence won't hurt, so long as you recognize that it *is* an indulgence and that you are going to let your grief dissipate when you feel you can, just as you let the crying for him go in its own time.

And there *is* a right time to let grief go. Some spiritualists and gurus strongly believe that grieving too long will stop your mate from getting on with his new life, because in those first months he is close by you, whether you can see or hear him or feel his presence or not. He will not leave until you are feeling better. But that holds him back when he has important things to achieve on a new agenda. That is one good reason for not staying miserable too long.

While no one but you can define 'too long,' it might happen that one day you will feel a little prick of guilt and realize that the pleasure has gone out of the crying, and that you are crying for crying's sake. That's the point at which you will feel like taking yourself in hand. You have gone through the rage and sorrow processes, and are reaching for the light. You find yourself counting your blessings instead of your problems. And sometimes you will feel like laughing.

Laughter is a magical part of the healing process. For a start, it is difficult to feel sorry for yourself and to have a good laugh at the same time. Secondly, the act of laughing releases a set of hormones called endorphins, which are actually pain suppressants, which is one of the reasons you feel so marvelous after a fit of laughter. There are documented cases of people who have literally laughed themselves back to health long after the doctors had given up hope. There is more than a little truth in the saying 'Laughter is the best medicine.'

I still remember the first real laugh I had after my husband's death. My family and I were watching a rather slow-paced television documentary on South Sea island tribal life. And to say that it was 'slow-paced' is being kind. The headman of the tribe was just about the saddest-looking individual you ever saw. For most of the show he sat, long-faced and cross-legged, with other male members of his tribe in a circle in the traditional cooking-pot-over-fire scenario. The camera crew left this riveting spectacle from time to time to zoom in on other nuggets of island life, but seemed compelled to return regularly for shots of the headman. Nothing much seemed to be happening. Each time he was captured on film, this chief was sitting staring solemnly at the pot. We were a bit mesmerized ourselves until my father quipped, 'Well, what a happy-looking fellow he is. Real life-of-the-party type.' The idea of this glum man ever being happy was so incongruous that each time the lens swooped in for yet another close-up, we cracked up. It felt good.

Along with laughing and crying comes talking. Talking is important, too. As with crying, there are two types of people: those who never stop talking, and others who keep their words tightly sealed in the same jar as their feelings.

In instances of shock and grief, talking is as important, and has as much therapeutic value, as crying and laughing. One good friend told me that she rarely got a chance to speak when her talkative and knowledgeable husband was alive. It was not until he died that she started talking; now she maintains that she surprises even herself with her volubility. But of course, *what* you talk about is as important as the act of talking itself, and what you should and probably want to talk about is your life with your mate. After all, weren't his opinions and philosophies important to you when he was alive? If they were, they will be especially so now. Another dear friend, who lives on the other side of the continent, bewailed the fact that she was not around to encourage me to talk.

Sometimes it does happen that your friends are not close by. If that is the case, and if you find it difficult to get out and about, there is always the telephone. I have a number of phone friends, people whom I rarely see for reasons of time or distance, but with whom the conversation is on just as intimate and enjoyable a basis as with those I see regularly.

And don't overlook talk radio as an opportunity for a hearty talk-fest. Reach out.

As well as talking about your mate, talk to him, too. Don't stop because he doesn't appear to be around. We don't know for certain that he's not—nobody really knows—and it is my personal belief, based on my studies and experience, that spirits do exist. They are as 'real' as you or me, but the vibratory dimension they exist within is different from ours, so we cannot see or touch them. But we can communicate.

As I have said, I found the best time to chat was in the privacy of my bedroom, either after I had gone to bed at night or when I first woke in the morning. Talk to your soul mate about your fears and concerns. Ask him to help to solve your problems. If you feel let down and deserted and mad at him for dying when he did, tell him so. After all, the chances are that you have been telling everyone how marvelous he was all day, so in the interests of honesty it won't hurt to adjust the scales a bit!

Talking through your problems is a well-proven psychological method of seeing things in a different perspective. It uncaps the press-seal jar, allows the emotions room to surface and, in doing so, allows their release.

So write or paste up your 'Let go' affirmation and take care to cry and laugh and talk as the opportunities present themselves. By doing this, you are working with your pain, not struggling against it, and you will find that it gradually starts to loosen its hold on you.

You can dispel the dark. Lighten up and see the beauty. Experience the fun. There are elements of fun and beauty in all we do each day.

Chapter Three

Being Gentle with Yourself

You can create for yourself
a garden of bliss
if you believe in it.

—*Emmanuel's Book*

Each week you must have a regular outing to look forward to, and each day you must do something you enjoy. This should be no hardship! And, as you do it, you will find that you are improving or adding to both the texture and structure of your life.

To start with, make your daily break something gentle with a 'peace factor' built in. It is important to do it regularly, so, if you are a busy person and tend to push things you regard as non-essential aside, make a note on your calendar or in your diary.

It is not always necessary to spend money to do things you enjoy. There is still a great deal you can do that is free for the asking. For example, if you enjoy walking—and live anywhere near a river or the sea—go for long daily walks by the water. Or go for a swim if that's possible. Water play in any form remains one of the world's great therapies. Allow thoughts of the water to fill your mind. Identify with it, gaze into it, feel it both in and outside yourself, make it part of you. If you are at the sea, think about the creatures that live in the ocean, about the yachts and liners and small craft that sail on it, about how the rays of the sun make it shake and shimmy or how the moon picks out a silvery path. Think of as many aspects of the water as you can. There is no need, for those few minutes, to think of anything else. Let your thoughts flow.

If you live in the country, you can enjoy roaming around the countryside. Vary the direction each day. Pick a posy of flowers for yourself. Lift your face to the sky and smile. Life is not so bad.

Even if you live in the city or suburbs without access to either water or country, you will usually find churches nearby. Whether or not you are a member of an organized religion, the peace you will get from spending half an hour or so inside a church will be worth any amount of effort you may have to make to get there. If you can get there by walking, so much the better, since you get the vital exercise factor built in.

Whether you are walking in the country, standing by the river or kneeling in church, take the pressure off yourself. If money worries are present, *believe* you will get that job, that you will find some way of paying the mortgage or even somewhere better to live. If your concern is your own health, go to Chapter Eleven, 'Quieting Your Mind and Body,' and start improving your health and your life from there. If you are worried that you are not coping well, relax. *Believe* that it will all work out. And it will.

As far and as often as your budget allows, pamper yourself. Looking good will help you to feel good.

Have your hair cut by the best salon you can afford. If you've always wanted to have your hair dyed or streaked, do it now. Visit a beauty salon for the luxury of a pedicure that will provide a bonus in relaxing your whole body, as well as an added benefit in the form of human touch, which is important.

Or book yourself in for an aromatherapy body massage. Massage is a very real aid to both your physical and mental well-being. As the blood is moved around your body, lymph nodes are drained, muscles are toned. A good massage will speed up the elimination of body wastes and poisons, and the aromatic oils will leave you feeling relaxed and invigorated and ready for just about anything.

If money is tighter than tight and something like a massage is a big luxury, trade your skills. For example, you may have a friend who is a masseur or beauty therapist who would be delighted to give you a treatment in exchange for your hemming and initialing towels for the salon, or distributing advertising fliers around town, or whatever your particular talent suggests. It works.

And so does indulging yourself with a long, hot, scented bath before bedtime.

Even if you have never been the hugging type, start hugging and allowing yourself to be hugged in return. My friend June is the huggiest person I know. She came up to me at a party three years ago and said, 'What you need is a hug.' That was the first of many warm and lingering hugs from that good woman that always leave me feeling loved no matter how I felt before. You will always get more out of a hug than you put in. Hugging costs nothing.

Being gentle with yourself means spending time both by yourself and with other people. Time with your own thoughts is important because there can be a lot to think through, and it is important that the thoughts surface and are acknowledged. So far, we've touched on what you can do on your own. But it is equally important to spend time with your friends, and to start meeting new people.

So instead of drinking too much tea or coffee at home, save the caffeine intake for a meeting with a friend. If you don't have a diary, invest in one now, and make sure that you make a minimum of two dates a week at your favorite café. If you are working, make dates for lunch or, if you feel up to it, dinner. Dress for the occasion.

This is the time, too, to decide on new sports, hobbies or interests. We are fortunate to live in a time when university extension services and various community centers offer classes in everything from learning computer languages to shoring up relations with a difficult neighbor. There are local clubs, specific-interest groups and sporting organizations, all looking for members. Any new interest or activity is as close, in most cases, as picking up the telephone and making a move. If you have always wanted to play golf, for example, but felt you never had the time or the talent, perhaps now you can check up on your talent levels and make the time. You may surprise yourself. There is nothing like the level of concentration that golf demands to take your mind off other things.

If you feel too shy to go along to a new venue on your own the first time, ask a friend to go along with you. One person I know started dancing classes several years ago and asked her girlfriend to accompany her for the first couple of outings. After that she was fine, and dancing has become one of the main focuses of her life in more ways than one. But whether you opt for guitar lessons once a week, a tai chi group for gentle exercise on a Saturday afternoon or local amateur theatricals, you will have something you enjoy to look forward to on a regular basis.

The advantages are many. A regular outing will get you out of your house or apartment, and that in itself will do wonders for your mindset. You will meet like-minded people and make new friends. You will learn a new hobby or sport, or improve a skill. You will reap the benefits of fresh air and exercise, improve the way you look and feel, and your attitude towards the world will gradually change.

An option that may present itself is travel. Personally, I believe that the act of staying put for a while, and filling in your diary with the fun things outlined above, is more beneficial in both the medium and long term because you are starting to rebuild the structure of your life in exactly the way you want it. This is a great opportunity that shouldn't be missed or taken lightly because, for many of us, much of life just happens without our being aware of deliberate choices. We wake up one day with lots of responsibilities and a haphazard structure that is many times not of our own conscious choosing. Now you have the time to sit down and lay the foundations for a new lifestyle, if that is your wish. Life may have been perfect before your mate died and you don't want it any different, but something we all have to accept is that *life is change*. According to one *hadith* (tradition), the prophet Muhammad maintained that to stay the same is not merely to be stagnant but is in fact a retrogressive step, since the world around us continues to move on. There is always something that can be added or improved.

If money is no problem and you don't have the responsibilities of children or pets, you might consider going away for a short time. However, I recommend saving bonafide travel—visiting far-flung and/or new places—for later, when you will get more out of it. But, if the opportunity presents itself, go to stay with a good friend by all means, preferably someone you have known for a long time who won't mind your chatting on ... and on ... and on.

Chapter Four

World of Words

Words which give peace, words which are good and beautiful and true, and also the reading of sacred books: this is the harmony of words.

—*Bhagavad Gita*

If you are a reader (and the fact that you are reading this book indicates that you might be), this is the time to read.

There are dozens of bookshops that cater specifically for readers of New Age literature and beyond. New Age, not so new any longer, incorporates books that cover the possibility that there is more to our life journey than the here and now we are endeavoring to handle on Earth. I find that thought both humbling and comforting. You will find books on mysticism, dreams, life after death, reincarnation, parallel lives, spiritualism, positive thinking, and whole new philosophies for effective living.

The works of the eighteenth-century philosopher and writer Emanuel Swedenborg center on the soul's existence after the death of its earthly body, and there is a conviction in his writings that is difficult to ignore. Swedenborg believed that when a person dies he or she is met by a host of friends and relatives who guide the recently deceased person in the new life. The now well-documented testimonies of the increasing number of people who have undergone Near Death Experiences (NDEs) in the late twentieth century bear uncanny resemblance to some of Swedenborg's descriptions of life after death. He maintained that if one partner dies before the other, as usually happens, the first partner will be waiting to greet his or her mate when that person's turn comes to die—akin to being met by your mate at an airport in our twentieth-century world. No more complicated and no more frightening. Swedenborg describes cities in the sky, everyone having a job or set of responsibilities, androgyny and no arguments. Sounds good to me!

Edgar Cayce, the famous American mystic who lived earlier this century, used to work by placing himself in a trance and making his predictions and forecasts from there. His words were faithfully written down by his secretary, Gladys Davis. Cayce believed that we are reincarnated several times and that the spell on Earth that we are currently undergoing is but one of many. He was of the strong opinion that kindred souls tend to reincarnate at roughly the same time so that the people we have known, loved or been related to in this life will be associated with us in one way or another in the next. Many Eastern religions believe similarly.

A special book for women is *Women Who Run with the Wolves* by Clarissa Pinkola Estés, which talks about the special powers of women, illustrated by dream analysis and myths and folk tales from all over the world. It is quite a fat book, and one of the few that I felt compelled to immediately start re-reading. One friend finds it works well for her as a bedside book she can dip into from time to time. It is enormously empowering.

Richard Bach of *Jonathan Livingston Seagull* fame has written several other delightful fictional books around the theme of soul mates, reincarnation and parallel lives. I liked both *The Bridge Across Forever*, in which he tells the real-life story of himself and his soul mate, and *Illusions*. American James Redfield's *The Celestine Prophecy* offers clever insights into the new waves of consciousness gradually being experienced by humanity. Ben Okri won the Booker Prize in 1991 for *The Famished Road*, a beautiful story that relates the wanderings of a spirit child, Azaro, in one of his incarnations on Earth.

Whatever your reading preferences or belief system, there is something for you. If you subscribe to the Judeo-Christian belief that it was our taste of the tree of knowledge that led to our lives on this imperfect Earth, well, now that we're here, let's make it a feast!

After reading comes writing, which, as a therapy, is right up there with the water play, laughing, crying, talking and hugging we discussed in the previous chapter.

Even if you have never tried, try writing something now—either poetry or prose—about how you are feeling and coping or not coping, as the case may be. Keep a notebook and pencil by your bedside and write as the urge takes you. You may be surprised how easily the words come, and a talent you never knew you had may emerge. At the very least, you will find that writing will 'cook' your emotions so that they are more palatable. In other words, the process of writing will help take away the rawness of the pain. The chances are, too, that you will find out more about yourself.

One of the best ways to incorporate the writing habit into your life is to keep a journal. This will be a book of any size, with lined pages that are undated. Record anything and everything important to you. Since it is undated, write only when you need to, which might be for seven consecutive days with a two-week break, or every morning and evening for a year. Tuck a pen or pencil into the book, so that it is always handy.

Into your journal write your concerns, joys, and sorrows. Write about the new sports, hobbies and interests that you are taking up, and why you are taking them up. Write about new books you have read or that have been recommended, and give them a critical review. Describe any unusual experiences, dreams, meditations and habits that you take on or drop off. Write about the people you know, their reactions, their friendship. Write about your family and their supportiveness or lack of same. Write about what is good in your life and what is bad, about the blessings and the lack thereof, about how you feel about God or the universe. Write your life forwards and backwards; in other words, describe the sets of circumstances that have brought you to this point in your life, and take a look at where you are going from here. Do you feel good or bad or indifferent at this time? Do you think things will change? And if they do, will it be for the better or for the worse? Why do you think that? Are you a lucky person or an unlucky person, and why? What is your attitude towards life, your friends, your family, the world? Does your attitude need changing? Have you ever considered your attitude before? Write about what you have to look forward to, and, if there is nothing, why not. And so on.

Get as close to the truth of your feelings as you possibly can. Some days you won't write in your journal. You will read it instead, and you will find the insights that you arrive at about yourself quite astounding. If there is nothing new, nothing astounding, perhaps you haven't been honest enough with yourself. Watching your own evolution is one of the most exciting hobbies there is.

I'd like to suggest that you resist the temptation to show your journal to anyone else. What you write in it should be an account of your deepest emotions, and should be written to be read only by yourself. That way you will have no subconscious reservations about what you write down. Your journal will not only be useful as a record of how you felt at this time, but you will be able to look back through it later to see how far you have moved away from the rough and tumble at the edges of the cyclone towards the peace at your center.

So whether you read or whether you write, or do a little or a lot of both, you will find that you are processing a great deal of new information that cannot help but move you ahead on your life journey.

Chapter Five

Coping with Your Sexuality

I am that fantasy which race has wrought
Of mundane chance-material. I am time
Paeaned by the senses five like bells that chime.

I am that cramped and crumbling house of clay
Where mansoul weaves the secret webs of thought.
Venturer—automan—I cannot tell
What powers and instincts animate and betray
And do their dreamwork in me. Seed and star,
Sown by the wind, in spirit I am far
From self, the dull control with whom I dwell.

Also I am ancestral. Aeons ahead
And ages back, both son and sire I live
Mote-like between the unquickened and the dead—
From whom I take, and unto whom I give.

—*Siegfried Sassoon*

The next few chapters have to do with coping with the changes that are going on in our lives, with the practical side of life that has to go on in spite of ourselves. Women in different age groups have different sets of problems to overcome when faced with the death of their partners (although the boundaries of these groups tend to blur or overlap). For example, although finances may be a problem for many of us, it is likely that young women will face greater monetary problems than those who are older and have had a chance to pay off their mortgages. Older women who have been married for a longer period may have more trouble overcoming their feelings of loneliness. And those in between may find among their greatest challenges the need to cope with teenagers as bewildered by events as they themselves are.

This chapter is directed to women who find, once the shock of their mate's death has worn off, that their sexuality has no ready outlet. In other words, the death of their partners has stopped their biological clocks—but only briefly. And then what do they do?

The fact that women need, and are entitled to, as full and as satisfying a sexual life as men still is not universally acknowledged. Female sexuality is cloaked in mystique—a bit like death. We see the female need for sex flaunted in the movies, we read about it in books, we experience the need ourselves, but still, our conditioning inhibits us from admitting that we have it.

If we admit its importance, might we not shed the mythical 'feminine mystique'? If we don't possess the mouth of Madonna, the body of Mae West or the madness of Glenn Close's character in *Fatal Attraction*, but instead happen to be an 'ordinary mother of two,' do we push our sexual desire to the back of the kitchen cupboard? Or do we allow it to surface naturally?

I believe your own body will tell you what to do.

Each of us is an individual, and needs vary considerably from person to person. Some may welcome celibacy, while others find that they possess the discipline to suppress their sexual energy and redirect that energy into work or sport. If you find the build-up of sexual energy not only physically distressing but mentally disturbing as well, a very real alternative is to masturbate. Set aside the old wives' tales, which are just that. If you masturbate, you will not go blind, and you will discover how to give yourself a great deal of pleasure. Whether they admit to it or not, the vast majority of men find it necessary to masturbate from time to time, and it is becoming more acceptable and accepted among women. If a healthy sexual urge is part of your nature and your man is missing from your life, don't frustrate yourself by abstaining. If you haven't got a clue about how to masturbate properly, off to the bookstore. Most good sex books have a chapter on masturbation, although if you have never done it before, you may have to persevere. Take time to learn about your own body. Take lots of time over several sessions, and don't stop until you achieve orgasm.

Vibrators are fun, and there are plenty to choose from, in every conceivable shape, size and color. If, like myself, you find the idea of sex-toy stores rather intimidating, taking a friend along could help break the ice. If there is no sex shop near you, or you don't fancy visiting one, buy a couple of erotic magazines and check out the ads. Most important, learn to improvise. You never knew your body could give such pleasure! And you won't believe how much better you function on all levels afterwards.

Finally, if the day should come—as impossible as it may seem right now—that you have the desire and opportunity to start building a new relationship, knowing your body better will make you a better lover. Meanwhile, during the recovery period that this book is addressing, our aim is to get back on track as soundly and solidly as possible, just as soon as we can.

Chapter Six

And What About the Children?

Your children are not your children.
They are the sons and daughters of
Life's longing for itself.

—*Kahlil Gibran*

In discussing children, I am aware that I am starting a chapter that does not really have an end. Generalities about how to deal with children's grief may not be of great help for your particular set of circumstances, but here are a few basic pointers to help the single parent reach out without panic, as well as some practical suggestions for mothers with young children.

I think that it helps to know that whatever you are experiencing with your children is *normal*. Under the circumstances behavioral changes are quite natural, and simply have to be dealt with in as constructive a manner as possible without adding to your own trauma or the trauma of your offspring.

My own children were in their middle and late teens when my second husband—not their father—died. Simply put, I don't know how I would have coped without them. My children, my extended family and my dogs were 'my

north, my south, my east and my west' in that initial period. There was no life beyond them. My son was overseas at
the time, but provided support that went way beyond his
sixteen years over the months following his return. On being
told I needed her, my seventeen-year-old daughter immediately canceled a trip to Hong Kong scheduled for the following day and flew the 'midnight horror' from one side of
Australia to the other to arrive in the north of Victoria late
the same afternoon. Each time I did a melty ice cream act,
she scooped me off the floor and set me moving again.

While teenagers will be teenagers and it is a rather
unsteady period at the best of times, the trauma that I
underwent obviously affected the children more than it had
to. In my ignorance, I passed my own fear of death onto the
next generation, causing a situation that will take years of
gentle counter-conditioning to redress. I am not suggesting
for a moment that we bottle up our feelings—there has been
enough damage done in that respect in the last two or three
generations—but that right from the start we bring our children up to respect the fact that death is part of life, that it is
the *jati-marana* that is part of all our destinies. I suggest that
through our own greater understanding of the cyclical
nature of life and death, we pass on our knowledge to our
children to enable them to put aside their own fears. It is
right that they should see our grief over our loss and that
they express their own grief over theirs. But it is also right
that they are shown that grief passes in its own time through
the understanding and acceptance of the nature of life.

While children can provide a marvelous mutual support
base, beware of leaning on them. When we lose a mate (and

this applies to divorce and separation, too), there is a tendency—albeit subconscious most times—to place more responsibility onto the children and demand more of them. Women who have lost the men in their lives may tend to lean on their sons. A friend of mine who didn't think she was demanding more than usual from her teenage son following her divorce realized, after a period of counseling, that in subtle ways she was. Once she changed her attitude to allow her son to take responsibility for himself, all his problems seemed to magically dissolve, not exactly overnight, but almost. Doubtless, I unconsciously put the same pressures on my own son.

Children are unlikely to say in so many words, 'Ease up, Mom,' so look for signs that you are leaning on them. Since your own actions may be too subtle to pick up, try reading the children instead.

Older children will rebel in smaller or greater ways, like playing truant from school, being late for dinner, shutting themselves in their rooms or forgetting to call to say they will be out late. Youngsters may become irritable, increase tantrum levels or show signs of internal anger by becoming destructive. One woman came home to find her five-year-old son working through the bookcase, systematically tearing up the books, one after another. Another woman was met with an icy aloofness from her hitherto warm and helpful teenage daughter.

In all cases, gentleness and understanding that we are not the only ones experiencing loss are required. But sometimes gentleness and understanding are not enough on their own. If you are experiencing difficulties with your children following the loss of their father, and the situation does not improve within a relatively short period of time, you need to seek professional advice. In the examples cited above, several short sessions with a qualified counselor were required before the respective situations returned to normal. If you do not know of an appropriate counselor, ask your church or your child's school or the local social services to refer you to the right person. If you live in the country and are unable to attend counseling sessions with your children, you may find one of the books recommended in the 'Further Reading' section at the end of this book to be helpful.

I tend to think that, whether the children are younger or older, women who have them to look after are perhaps more fortunate than those who do not. Being forced to think about mundane everyday tasks like shopping, preparation of meals, allowances and homework provides a good start to the rebuilding of structure we discussed in Chapter Three, 'Being Gentle with Yourself.' If you have youngsters screaming for attention as you read this, you will be unlikely to agree. There is no doubt that having children to support can impose extra strain on your own already stretched resources—physical, mental and financial.

One strategy here is to take things a day at a time. Start by counting your blessings. Once over the initial difficulties that readjustment always brings but which do pass, your children will remain as a tangible manifestation of the love you and your mate shared together. You will want to do things with them and for them, *without leaning*. If your dual role is at first a burden, you will adjust, and the bond that is forged during this time will be hard to break.

From a purely practical point of view, if you find yourself getting irritable with the children, particularly young children, take full advantage of friends and family. Farm the children out for a morning or for a couple of hours while you have a much-needed break to do some shopping or pamper yourself, as described in Chapter Three.

If you have toddlers too young for preschool or kindergarten, and are in a situation where you do not have family or friends to call on for child care, why not start a play group? A play group costs virtually nothing to run, and the free time you gain outweighs the input by four to one. I know. I tried it for a hugely successful two years when both my children were toddlers.

A play group works on strictly reciprocal lines. Ideally it consists of five parents who take turns looking after their five children for one morning a week each. The system works best, of course, if all parents stick conscientiously to the day they have been allotted.

The most obvious advantage to the plan is the four free mornings a week you will reap for the input of one morning's effort. If you have two children, you might put in an extra morning's work here and there, or 'cover' for a mother who cannot make it one day. Another very real benefit is the knowledge that your child is being securely looked after and actively stimulated at the same time, which is loads better for the child than tagging around after a busy, preoccupied and not-very-happy mom all morning.

Becoming a play group mom will take away the pressure of young demands for several mornings a week, allow you valuable free time and provide the comfort of knowing that you are doing your best for your children at the same time. There is also the bonus of meeting other parents in your age group who may later become good friends.

For the children, it is win-win all the way. A play group is a chance to mix regularly with other children in a constructive manner. They learn to share their parents, their toys and their homes, and in return get to play with a variety of toys in other homes. They also learn to respect the rules of each household. Mixing with other children and being apart from mother in a happy environment also bodes well for their introduction to preschool or kindergarten. And a big plus comes in the fact that in making new friends, their attention is diverted from their recent loss.

To get your group going, start by asking friends and acquaintances of preschoolers. Secondly, place a card on your local church, supermarket or laundromat bulletin board asking for volunteer parents within your area. Or, if you can get your neighborhood newspaper to run a story on play groups and mention that you need another couple of moms to make it viable, I guarantee you will have enough members for several groups, as I very quickly found when I tried it. Good luck.

Chapter Seven

Eradicating Loneliness

Autobiography in Five Short Chapters

1

I walk down the street.
There is a deep hole in the sidewalk.
I fall in.
I am lost ...I am hopeless.
It isn't my fault.
It takes forever to find a way out.

2

I walk down the same street.
There is a deep hole in the sidewalk.
I pretend I don't see it.
I fall in again.
I can't believe I'm in the same place.
But it isn't my fault.
It still takes a long time to get out.

3

I walk down the same street.
There is a deep hole in the sidewalk.
I see it is there.
I still fall in ... it's a habit.
My eyes are open.
I know where I am.
It is my fault.
I get out immediately.

4

I walk down the same street.
There is a deep hole in the sidewalk.
I walk around it.

5

I walk down another street.

—Portia Nelson

In leading what can only be called an itinerant life, I believe I have come to know a lot about loneliness and solitude, and the difference between the two states.

To me, loneliness is something you experience when you wish you were not experiencing it. Loneliness has a feeling of impotence about it. It is an emptiness that you feel when someone close to you leaves or dies, or when you yourself move away. Having undergone nearly fifty changes of address in eleven different countries, I feel I know a lot about loneliness, about leaving the people I love or get along well with, and making new friends. When my mate died, I was beset by another type of loneliness. We had lived for each other, and I missed him badly. It took a long time for the loneliness to dissipate. Loneliness is a state of being that I would never choose.

Solitude is different. Solitude implies that we do have a choice in whether or not we want to be alone. And at times we all have a need to be alone. I certainly do. One of my favorite treats to myself is to curl up in bed on a rainy winter's afternoon with a cup of tea, a green apple and a good book. That's a little glimpse of what heaven could be like. Or lying on a rug in the garden looking up through the tree branches with my dogs snoring on the grass beside me. Or reading the newspaper in a crowded street café, enjoying my solitude within the noisy laughing crowd. Solitude is a gentle state, an interim state between periods of contact with others. It provides time to get to know oneself, to think, to read, to walk, to meditate, to be.

Solitude is choosing to be alone. Loneliness is something that is thrust upon us, sometimes when we least expect it.

I have found that it is possible, with a little effort, to eradicate loneliness and welcome solitude in its place. It is possible to change a situation over which you have no control into one where you call the shots. You want the right to decide if and when and where you want to be alone, and if and when and where you want company. You also want the right to decide which type of company you wish to associate with.

Merely surrounding yourself with people is not necessarily the answer. Big cities and bad marriages have a lot in common. On the other hand, it pays to start off by getting to know lots of people; the law of attrition will apply in its own time.

I have found that there are two major steps involved in winning the right to choose when and where you want to be alone: that of attitude and that of action. A lot of loneliness comes from having a negative attitude. This gives rise to such comments as 'There's no one I can relate to here,' or 'I'm only

going to be here for a short while, so why bother,' or 'I'm dull
and boring, so why would anyone want to make friends with
me anyway?' Because these thoughts and comments are self-
defeating, you are beaten before you start. A negative attitude
needs to be challenged by some positive thinking. And then
it is time to take action. There is no point in having your attitude in the right place if you then take no action.

Take attitude first.

As distinct from the healthy crying that promotes the
release of tension, the feeling-sorry-for-myself-nobody-
loves-me act that we all slip into from time to time simply
doesn't work in terms of getting the type of attention we
need and deserve as human beings. If 'poor me' becomes a
habit, we slip into martyrdom. This manifests itself in nothing seeming 'to go right.'

I'm sure you have experienced times when everything
goes wrong compared with the other times when the sun
seems to shine on everything you do. It is time to ask yourself whether it is an accident or a coincidence that everything goes wrong at once. It is time to wonder at the fact
that some days the phone rings off the hook and other days
stays silent. It is time to take a look at your attitude, how
you are feeling and acting when events and situations
around you are not to your liking.

Are you calm and accepting, knowing that the only thing
you can control on Earth is you, and that other people and
outside events are beyond your immediate control? Do you
regard yourself as a lucky person? Or do you rage, get
depressed or moan that it (it being the nasties) always happens to you?

Since life is balance—the yin and the yang—you will be served plenty of both, the good and the not-so-good, and will thus have ample time to assess your own attitude both *before* 'things started going right or wrong' and *during* the process.

As one of the acknowledged leaders of the human potential movement, author and lecturer Stuart Wilde writes in *The Force*:

> You have infinite potential as your birthright and nothing should stand in your way. You are an individual. You have been incarnated here to understand yourself, and a part of doing so is learning to relate to others, your family and loved ones, but eventually it comes down to you on your own. You do not have a responsibility for the growth of others. ... Many people sit around waiting for the world to discover them and that rarely happens. If you move toward your goals, expressing all your power, opportunity will find you as a result of your actions.

Your goal is to make friends. And if you already have friends, make more friends. Be broad in your approach. Set arrogance and ego aside and be friendly to everyone. Closer friendships tend to arise when you feel alive and stimulated in the other person's company and when you have something in common with each other. But don't restrict yourself in your search. There are many different types of friendship, and all are valuable in their own right. Some friends are made at school or at a young age and are still around decades later; others are formed from compatible interests; others are friends who have held each other's hands through crises but who may not have much in common. Then there are work friends, phone friends and pen pals. There are friends whom you enjoy meeting for a coffee or a game of tennis, people who are more than acquaintances. And then there are closer friends: those in front of whom you can let down all the barriers, forget the pretenses and the make-believe. Close friendship is something that is forged—like iron or steel—and takes its shape, like all forging, when the heat is on. But, close or not so close, real friends like you for you. Real friends are there when you need them. It is easy to be around people when all is going well for them; it is less easy to share their sorrows. Some of my greatest friendships were forged following the death of my husband, and today there are no words adequate to describe how much they mean to me. If you know that merely by picking up the phone or dropping in on someone you don't have to be alone, the loneliness disappears.

Once, in the lonely desertscape of Arabia, I was told that in life we need but one good friend. I have not found that to be so. Rather, I believe that in life, we need as many good friends as we have time and energy to do the right thing by. The reality of life is that people die, move away, go on vacation, retreat from us and change. To expect one good friend to be always on hand is unrealistic.

So, how do you make friends, the real friends you are after, not just people who fill in time for each other? One answer is to put into operation the techniques mentioned earlier. Moving away from loneliness needs that two-part mix: a change of mental attitude if you are stuck in the 'poor-me' mode, plus the physical effort involved in actively moving towards your goal.

First, if you don't yet have one, develop and practice a friendly and open attitude towards people. That means showing a genuine interest in others while becoming aware of your own ego, and gradually eradicating any offputting behavior such as arrogance or being overly critical. While mental attitude is not something that can be changed overnight, there are many spiritual and mental-health centers and teachers available all across the country, as well as many excellent books on the subject of attitude, some of which are listed at the back of this book. Once you start on the journey towards getting to know yourself better— although it may take a little while to get things going smoothly in the direction of your choice, and you may falter a number of times—essentially you are moving towards your goal. To me, the wonderful little poem called 'Autobiography in Five Short Chapters' quoted at the beginning of this chapter says it all.

The physical effort involved in overcoming loneliness is perhaps for many people less complex than tackling attitudinal problems. Take action by doing something. Don't allow a potentially lonely day to just descend on you. Plan to have coffee with a friend, treat yourself to a massage or start a new novel. For ongoing action, join a club or an organization, take a course (and when that finishes, take another), take up a sport, learn to play chess or bridge, or offer your help to one of the hundreds of charities desperately in need of volunteers.

If you are confined to home, cultivate phone friends, offer your services to a social-services hotline, send letters by E-mail to people in distant lands, have people to your home to play cards or music, start a book club—your choices are as wide as your own ingenuity and level of energy.

Having animal companions at home is also a great way for you to counteract loneliness. Depending on your living circumstances and degree of mobility, you might consider giving a home to one of the dogs or cats awaiting their fate at the local ASPCA. Or buy a bird feeder and leave food for the birds each morning. Nurturing plants can also help, as any gardener knows. After the separation from my first husband in Hong Kong, I underwent what can only be described as an extremely depressing period in a dark and dingy flat that happened to face a mountain, regarded as bad *feng shui* in those parts. An instant lift to my living conditions, and thus to my attitude and morale, came when my sister arrived on a visit, took one look and went out to buy a host of brightly colored cushions and leafy plants. The plants lent life where it had been missing before, and I was never lonely there again.

What you don't do is sit on your hands and wait for time to pass. Do things. And if you are in a frame of mind where there is nothing you want to join, play, learn or take up, spare a thought for those less well off mentally, physically or financially than yourself. Figure out ways you can help them, and volunteer your services.

Perhaps it was not meant that we should ever know all the secrets of the universe. But one thing is proven beyond a doubt: if you reach out by helping yourself first, then others, the bounty you will reap will be way beyond any money or effort you have expended. As author Wayne Dyer says, 'You'll see it when you believe it.'

So, you see, there is really no need to sit at home experiencing loneliness. It is something that you have the power to change. Loneliness can be eradicated and interspersed with voluntary periods of solitude. You will find beauty in your own thoughts, and comfort in the sounds of the silences. You will be aware of, and able to enjoy, the serenity of being on your own and the stimulation of having the right company at the right time. You do have a choice, but only you can activate that choice.

Chapter Eight

The Practical Side of Carrying On

The manner with which we work through change
determines whether it be stress or stimulus.

—Julian Boul Noies

God give us grace to accept with serenity the things that cannot
be changed, the courage to change the things which should be
changed, and the wisdom to distinguish the one from the other.

—Reinhold Niebuhr

In periods of peak emotion, of major life events like death, it is often assumed that practical matters will take care of themselves. Sometimes that does happen, but it is certainly not always the case. Whatever our attitude or state of mind regarding the death of a partner, there are certain things that have to be done that are difficult primarily because we have never done them before.

Many of us have never been to a funeral, let alone been involved in the organization of one. This can be quite challenging when you are feeling wobbly.

If the concept and discussion of death were not so shunned in our society, we would talk about death with our partners throughout our lives, not as something to be dreaded but as something that is inevitable for both of us. We would discuss the pros and cons of cremation versus burial, religious preferences, and the practicality of funeral costs. We would question whether we wish to be buried in the same grave as our partner, or whether we want our ashes scattered on a river; whether we want a funeral, and how large a gathering we envisage. And if either, or both, of us want a full-scale funeral, is the money pre-paid or securely locked away for that purpose? And then, and this is the important part, having made these decisions, we would *write them down somewhere accessible* to both parties and to our offspring. If you have already done the talking, and life and death are in front of you both, regard it as imperative to record the information, and file it somewhere you can find it—with your respective wills, if you have wills, or with the house mortgage or passports or citizenship papers, if you do not.

You may think you know your mate and *his* mind, but funerals take place as soon after death as possible, and while you may have known his mind, your mind may be temporarily on holiday.

These are matters that we would sort out if death were not regarded with such fear, if we did not feel that, by the simple act of talking about such things, we were somehow bringing the event closer. If you happen on this book early enough, do both yourself and your mate a favor by getting all of the above sorted out early on, and update it as time goes by. You will be saving both of you many unnecessary hassles.

One of the choices with which you are faced is whether or not to pre-pay funeral expenses. Caution should be exercised here, as such arrangements are often used as a pretext for later adding on to the costs of the funeral and burial, or to refuse a refund when the consumer wishes to cancel the pre-payment agreement (in the case, say, of a change of residence). Both the Continental Association of Funeral and

Memorial Societies and the American Association of Retired Persons recommend consulting a lawyer before finalizing any pre-payment agreement. As an alternative to pre-payment, you may want to consider placing equivalent funds in an interest-bearing savings account, credit-union account or other safe investment.

How to dispose of your mate's physical remains is a highly personal decision that may be influenced by any number of considerations, including the relative expenses involved. Although cremation followed by a memorial service will generally run less than earth burial, opting for a full funeral with your loved one's body present prior to cremation will tend to equalize costs. My mother donated her body to a university for research purposes, and my father wishes to do likewise. Most medical schools will see to disposal of the remains—and will, if requested, return the ashes to the family, although this may entail a delay of a year or more.

While the cost of 'immediate burial' or 'direct cremation' (that is, without a funeral service) may be as little as $1,000, for conventional burial or cremation—which includes the costs for conducting the funeral, the casket, and burial or cremation—you have to be prepared to spend from about $5,000 upwards. There is no ceiling on the upwards—the casket alone can cost up to $30,000—and you should be aware that $5,000 buys very little. Other costs—for such things as a donation or payment to the priest or minister or celebrant, piper or organist, notices in the paper, flowers or wreaths and gravestone or plaque—are all extra. Grave markers can cost from about $300 upwards, and you are usually required to wait for a few months before having it installed. You write your own message and pay by the word. If the message is especially original, it may have to be approved by the cemetery concerned.

If you haven't the money for all this, don't panic. There are sources of help—depending, of course, on eligibility. If your mate was a military veteran, you may be eligible for death benefits (towards funeral, burial, cemetery plot and headstone costs) from the Department of Veterans' Affairs (see 'U.S. Government' pages near the front of your telephone directory). The U.S. Social Security Administration publishes a pamphlet for 'Survivors,' which you may obtain at a local office or by telephoning their toll-free number: (800) 772-1213. Other potential sources of financial assistance include benefits from trade unions and fraternal orders, employee benefits, credit-union protection plans, church mutual-aid plans and, of course, life insurance policies.

If you have been named executor in your partner's will, it is your responsibility to notify his bank of his death. Enclose a death certificate with the notification. As far as joint bank accounts are concerned, you are at liberty to draw out all or part of the money at any time. The bank does prefer, however, that the joint account be closed following the death of a partner, and a new one opened in your name. If a lawyer is employed as administrator to settle the estate—this may well be the case if there is no will appointing a specific executor—his or her fees (and, in fact, any legal expenses incurred in protecting your rights to taxable income) can be claimed as a legal deduction against your own tax liabil-ity. ('Estate,' by the way, is the rather elevated term given to any property or assets owned by the deceased. Even a savings book with a balance of $100 constitutes 'estate.')

Another practical matter is whether or not to stay in the same house or dwelling. If you have children at local primary schools, or are closely involved with your local community, and if your partner has left you comfortably provided for, you may derive more benefit from staying put than from moving away.

Test your feelings for a little while before making any major move. If you are now at a stage where you will be living alone with a too-large house and garden to worry about, you may prefer to move to an apartment where you have more time to enjoy yourself, and where security is less of an issue.

We are all different and our needs will vary, but be prepared: *everyone* will give you advice—particularly on the moving issue—and their suggestions will range from one end of the spectrum to the other.

One woman took the advice of her friends and stayed in the family home for twelve months following the death of her husband before leaving to rent an apartment for herself. She remembers the year with horror. 'I seemed to leave an echo in every room,' she recalls. 'In the end, I was in a fever to get out. Staying put did nothing for my morale, and, with hindsight, it was not a good decision from any point of view.' Another woman takes great pride in recalling how she slept in the same bed by herself right from the first night, and maintains that by 'taking the pain like bad medicine all in one dose' she recovered more quickly. Another woman moved from house to retirement village, where she has made a heap of new friends of both sexes, taken up with great success hobbies she felt she had 'only toyed with for ages,' and is finding life not only busy but exciting and challenging, too.

A final practical measure that should not be overlooked is the making of a will. You may have made joint or separate wills while your husband was still alive. If not, your partner is said to have died 'intestate,' which only means that he died without leaving a will. If there is time to prepare a will (joint or otherwise), you should do so now. Otherwise, you should ensure that you make your own will when you feel up to it. A will is an essential piece of paper without which only the lawyers make money. It saves a great deal of time, money, mental and physical energy, not to say family disagreements and heartbreak. Whether you are a multimillionaire with megabucks spread worldwide or have little more to leave than your potted plants, you should regard making a will as a necessity.

To prepare a will, you may wish to hire a lawyer or invest in a do-it-yourself will book or software package. Be sure to update your will as circumstances change—as now, for example, with the death of your mate. Or when you acquire or sell property, a car or expensive jewelry. Provision for pets can also be made in your will. Be aware that if you remarry, you need to make another will.

While there is no doubt that having plentiful reserves of money makes all this organization easier in the short term, in the long term this is not necessarily so. To be able to put as much physical space between yourself and your loss as possible—to be able to fly off to distant lands without a care in the world, for example—makes it seem as if money is important. From the experiences I have observed, however, this is not necessarily so.

Pain is pain and has to be worked through, whoever you are and however much wealth you have. Merely placing a physical distance between yourself and the cause of the pain does not necessarily lessen the emotional loss. While flying away or spending money may certainly help as a distraction in the short term, you can make yourself just as busy by working out ingenious ways to continue to provide your children with their allowances if you have less cash than you need for the moment.

The most important thing to remember is to do what is right for you and the people in your care within the parameters of your energy and finance levels.

Chapter Nine

Dreaming

Trust the dreams, for in them is hidden
the gate to eternity.

—*Kahlil Gibran*

People who remember their dreams can get as passionate about dreaming as sports fans do about their favorite sports, while those with no more than a passing interest in either wonder what all the fuss is about.

For psychologist Carl Jung the dream was

> a little hidden door in the innermost and most secret recesses of the soul, opening into that cosmic night which was psyche long before there was any ego-consciousness, and which will remain psyche no matter how far our ego-consciousness extends.

He went on to say:

> Dreams are neither deliberate nor arbitrary fabrications; they are natural phenomena which are nothing other than what they pretend to be. They do not deceive, they do not lie, they do not distort or disguise, but naively announce what they are and what they mean.

Unlike his predecessor Sigmund Freud, who believed that dreams are almost always connected to the experiences of our waking life, Jung believed that dreams have a significance far greater than anything that could be produced by the conscious mind. For Freud, dreaming was the result of an overload of a busy life, and connected with past, rather than future, events. For Jung, dreams provided a link with the spirit or soul.

American mystic Edgar Cayce was another who believed that dreams are connected with the psyche or the unconscious. Cayce saw dreams as the 'nightly channel of the higher self.' He believed that as we fall asleep our body relaxes, our conscious mind dissolves and our sixth sense, or 'intuition,' takes over. It is out of that sleep of 'pure intuitive being,' that our soul awakens.' As other eminent scholars, including contemporary psychotherapist Scott Peck, conduct experiments into the art of dreaming, Freud's view becomes progressively outdated.

If you dream a lot, and are interested enough to conduct your own investigations into whether your dreams are merely an 'overload' of a busy mind or carry a weightier and more exciting significance, the bookstores carry a range of books on dreaming. I have listed some favorites in the 'Further Reading' section at the end of this book. And if you live in or near a city, you may be able to find a center that offers courses in understanding and interpreting dreams. I went to dream school about three months after the death of my husband and found the group analysis a great experience in terms of linking my dream world with everyday life.

Before you do anything else, keep a record of your dreams, and then reflect on them from time to time during the day. Symbols presented to you in a dream—and I tend to favor Jung's theory that they come up from the subconscious—need to be acknowledged, however briefly, during the day. For example, if you have a particularly vivid dream about a red dress, merely bring it to mind while dressing in the morning or when you come across the color red. You may not understand at first what the dream is trying to tell you, but it is important to acknowledge the dreamworld, important to say, 'I hear you'. Dreams that seem particularly obtuse will often be repeated using different symbols if the message is significant enough.

Your journal is an ideal place to write down your dream experiences. Records I have kept over the last few years map an interesting path in terms of my psychic self.

Some people say they do not dream. We all do, though some people do not remember their dreams on waking. If you are in the latter category, try the technique of catching what I call the 'tail' of a dream on waking. If you do this and can trace back the last few incidents, you may be able to recall a lot, although I have to admit that it is a bit like climbing up a slippery snake backwards. Freud suggests that we forget our dreams because they aren't necessarily presented to us in the ordered manner we are used to in our waking life. He draws the analogy of a verse: 'If a short line of verse is divided up into its component words and these are mixed up, it becomes very hard to remember.' Although this line of reasoning drew argument from his colleagues, anyone who has ever tried to remember a sentence in its entirety, then in the same number of words but jumbled, might agree with Freud.

As a practical step to remembering, I suggest you keep a pen and a dream notebook by your bed so that when you do have a dream you can catch by the tail, you can record it immediately. It will not be long before you are remembering more and more. Conversely, if you dream copiously and wake up remembering most or all of your dreams, don't try to write them all down. You may find yourself spending a large part of your day recording the events of the night before! Instead, record only the most vivid dreams or those you consider the most significant, and your dreamworld will settle back to an acceptable level. It is the quality, not quantity, of your dreams that is important.

Another problem you may have with your dreams is that they don't always 'announce what they are and what they mean' in quite such a concise manner as Jung would have us believe. My cousin Neil Wylde puts it this way: 'The message is always clear; sometimes it is the language that the dream is cloaked in that is not. A dream talks in symbols and it is a matter of understanding the symbols.'

There are some symbols that are accepted as fairly standard by a number of sources and this will become clear as your work on your dreams progresses. For example, a car is generally regarded as an expression of your personality; water in a dream represents emotionalism; dreams in which family members participate are often representations of the self. Males in your dream may be symbols of your persona or the character that you present to the world, versus your real self.

A word of warning here: beware of books that set out to decipher dream symbolism dictionary-style. What means something for one person does not necessarily mean the same thing for another, and it is important to work on the dream itself as a whole, not as a collection of separate symbols. Take the pressure off, and for the most part the dreams themselves will do the work. The most important dreams will make themselves known to you in follow-up dreams that might use a completely different set of symbols to get their message across. It is widely held that the dream you have just before waking is the most important.

Once you become adept at reflecting on the significance of your dreams, you will find that they will provide a useful insight into your current state of mind. Besides, they're fun, and a great improvement on television!

It was through the medium of dreaming that Jung considered that a 'scientific contribution [had been made] to the problem of death, or of life after death.' For Jung, the experiments into the 'phenomena of true dreams' by J. B. Rhine in the United States furnished the particular 'scientific proof' he required for life after death. He became convinced that through the process of dreaming 'the psyche at least partially extends into the realm of relative or even absolute timelessness and spacelessness.' This takes us back to the discussion in Chapter One, 'Understanding Death,' on how the language we speak molds our perception of human time.

Chapter Ten

Relating to Other People

Two men looked out from prison bars
One saw the mud, the other saw stars.

—Thelma Thompson

Other people. Without them, where would we be? Equally, I'm sure we sometimes ask ourselves: With them, where are we?

Other people are the warp to our weft, the cross-threads of our existence without which the fabric of our life cannot help but fall apart. We need people. People need us. It's a two-way situation (see Chapter Seven, 'Eradicating Loneliness'). We draw into our lives the people we need for one reason or another, usually to keep us moving along on our journey by either prodding or supporting.

Sometimes, however, we feel that we can do without other people. We meet someone in the street who expresses awkwardly her sympathy over our loss. Instead of making us feel better, it makes us want to cry. We stiffen up, hold back the emotions, and move on as quickly as possible. We are out of sorts for the rest of the day, and a small part of us feels that the other person was to blame. Why couldn't she have simply greeted us and moved on?

A few things are going on here. In the first place, we are given in life what we need at the time, whether we acknowledge that or not. If we hold the sorrow or the anger in and let the increasing tension build so that we feel progressively worse as the day wears on, this is our responsibility and not that of the passerby. The emotional tension that has been building has been given an opportunity to release itself. How we deal with this, or whether or not we take advantage of that opportunity, is up to us.

Secondly, part of living in society is to be aware of and sensitive to other people's emotions, their own possible embarrassment, their wish to help, their often fumbling attempts to communicate. Remember that our society regards death with fear, horror and dismay. To a greater or lesser extent, our friends and acquaintances are mirrors—or projections—of ourselves, our feelings, our embarrassment. The only thing we can do is to be honest with both them and ourselves. If you genuinely feel fine, happy and light-hearted at the very moment someone comes up to you and expresses her sympathy, tell her so. If you feel leaden and depressed, say so. If you feel like crying, dancing or having a cup of coffee, do it. And if you are unable to say or do anything at all, that's all right, too. At the same time, allow your sense of fair play full rein. The street is not the place to launch into a list of what isn't going right at that particular moment. Just get as close to your own feelings as a sensitive appreciation of time and place allows, and you will find that it helps.

Often we sense that we are picking up on another's embarrassment, when in fact their reaction is only a mirror of how we are feeling ourselves. Most people—and fortunately I rarely come across the other sort—really want to be of help. It is just that, sometimes, our human condition gets in the way of our saying what we feel. If you see someone struggling for expression and not quite getting there, perhaps it's a signal to move away from self-involvement and help them out.

From time to time, people have expressed concern about whether sending sympathy or condolence notes is a positive or a negative move. They wonder whether such messages might aggravate the loss and whether it might not be better to treat the bereaved person in as 'normal' a manner as possible. The only way I find to answer that is to say that, while death should not be regarded as in any way 'abnormal,' at the same time the bereaved person is experiencing shock and loss. To acknowledge that fact is to treat her in a normal manner. Expressing sympathy is normal. Anything that helps to alleviate the hurt is positive. To know that there are other people out there who sympathize with your situation and care about what you are going through is pretty fine stuff. It is possible that a word of sympathy or a card will reopen a healing wound, but wounds that heal quickly from the outside-in can cause trouble later on. Far better that the hurt and sadness are thoroughly drained from the very beginning.

As for sending sympathy cards, flowers or whatever, I believe that people should do what they feel moved to do. Anything done only out of a sense of duty or responsibility, or with any hint of a grudge attached to it, cannot help but come over in just that way to the recipient.

I found both the letters of sympathy and the cards deeply moving and, in many ways, a joyous experience, spinning round me a cocoon of warmth when I most needed it. To me, they were evidence that others outside my immediate circle of family and close friends cared how I felt. It was their way of sharing the experience with me. One woman whom I did not know very well at the time sent such a genuine letter of concern that a wonderful friendship with her and her husband developed, and deepens as the years go by.

One thing that gave me occasion for thought was the way in which other people appeared to view the timespan following the death of my husband. When, in answer to one woman's question of how long I had been on my own, I replied, 'Well over a year'—thinking what a long fifteen months it had been—I was surprised at her counter-response, 'Oh, it was that recent?' Actually, I was more than surprised— I was shocked. The comment pressed all sorts of guilt buttons within me as to whether I should have been at the dinner at all, or whether it would have been more 'proper' to have remained at home with the dogs. I find it interesting that five years later the response remains similar—'Oh, that's not long, is it?'—so I tend to feel that other people's opinion of what is long and what is not long is irrelevant so far as I am concerned.

Time is but time, as I said earlier, and it depends on how you use that time whether you are going to feel buoyant or depressed six months, one year, ten years or fifty years down the track. Our lives are in our own hands.

I also rebel at the terms 'widow' or 'widower.' Both words seem to me archaic, and this is the only mention that you will find in this book. The words are depressing in themselves, and cumbersome and unnecessary in today's world.

While we need other people and the wider world they create around us, it is up to us to take full responsibility for our lives, and to stand and face that world squarely. If suggestions are made to us with which we are not comfortable, or if we are placed in categories that neither suit nor fit us, or if other people are pulling the strings that make us dance to the wrong tune, it is up to us to be sensitive to the alarm bells that ring inside us. And to gently, but firmly and insistently, speak up or take action.

Chapter Eleven

Quieting Your Mind and Body

The mind is its own place, and in it self
Can make a Heav'n of Hell, a Hell of Heav'n.

—*John Milton*

The still revolutionary insight of Buddhism is that life and death
are in the mind, and nowhere else.

—*Sogyal Rinpoche*

If your mind is a wild thing that refuses to listen to you, then you need to do something about it. Don't just stand by and let the stress build as your life slips out of control, but think about taking a course in mental discipline, or quieting your mind and body, as soon as possible. I use these terms to cover a wide range of available options, from meditation to yoga to positive thinking.

How to get started? Contacting someone you know or who is recommended is probably the best idea for the simple reason that, unfortunately, not all practitioners in these areas are qualified: it is a sad fact that the so-called spiritual world is no freer of the occasional shady operator than other businesses and professions. By asking for a referral from someone whose judgment you respect, you obviate these hazards and are more likely to find the type of person best qualified for your particular needs. If you haven't explored this area of your life before, and neither your children nor friends can help, try asking at your local metaphysical bookstore or among people working in allied areas—like the woman who gave you the aromatherapy massage that relaxed you so much. Failing this, you can check the various alternative newspapers for details of upcoming courses and convenient venues. But do check credentials. It is most important to find someone you can trust.

Listed below are different types of mental discipline or centering processes, one or another of which I have found helpful at different stages over the last few years. Meditation has been a faithful standby for me for a long time, and in combination with, say, Reiki, helps to tap into that store of knowledge that tells us that we are but one small part of something wonderful and incredibly powerful. There is no need to feel small and alone. Help is as close as reaching out, and these practices provide a means of reaching out. Regular use of any one of them may result in replacing hot panicky feelings with a sense of stability and the knowledge that you are not alone.

MEDITATION

If you do not already meditate, it is worth considering building the habit into your daily life. To be beneficial, meditating should become as automatic and as regular as cleaning your teeth or feeding your pet.

The benefits of meditation are wide-ranging and long-lasting. Meditation will help reduce stress, lower your pulse rate and your blood pressure, and help give your mind the peace it craves. Practiced in conjunction with other therapies like Reiki or psychotherapy, it will help clear the psychic toxins from your body. It will enable you to stand back a bit from the harried pace of things and allow you to take control of your life instead of being at the mercy of stormy circumstance. There is little to stand in the way of regular meditation practice: it costs nothing in terms of money and will occupy no more than twenty minutes—or 1/72—of your day. Lastly, don't rush to the mirror, but in six weeks' time or so, you may find that you both look and feel younger. Instead of your face having a screwed-up, harassed, put-upon look, it will radiate peace from the inside out. Instead of your rushing around from place to place, putting—you think—lots into life and getting comparatively little back for your efforts, you will find you present a more peaceful, collected version of yourself to the world, which, in the universe's own time, will be reciprocated. You will have started to connect with your center.

There are two people currently in my life who, to me at least, appear to be well on the way to achieving a true state of inner peace and connectedness. Neither of these people would maintain that they were 'enlightened' to any great extent; on the contrary, they would insist they are all too human. But they both engage in regular meditation, and it manifests in radiating peace and love. It is not necessary for me to be in the physical presence of these people to connect with the peace that is theirs; merely talking to them on the phone seems to highlight the difference between our states of energy. I feel drawn into a sense of perfect peace. This, then, is the calm center of the cyclone, the serenity towards which we, as humans, are striving.

There are many different types of meditation, and your local library or bookstore will be able to help you out with books and tapes.

So far as my own meditation practice is concerned, I like to keep it simple. The idea behind meditation is to clear the mind, to free it from the clutter of everyday problems by concentrating on a single thought, sound or idea. Or, as you progress, to concentrate on the gaps between the thoughts and just *be*.

If you decide you would like to start meditating regularly, think about the best time for your meditation. Pick a time of day or night when you are least likely to be disturbed. I find morning best, just after waking while my cup of tea is cooling to a drinkable temperature; some people prefer the evening before sleep, their rationale being that the peace engendered by the mental exercise ensures a sound sleep. Fit in an extra meditation at any time during the day when you are feeling tired, stressed or in need of a lift.

It is best to meditate sitting up—with a straight back and cross-legged if you can—either in bed or on the carpet or in a favorite nature spot. In this way, you are aligning your energy from the earth upwards. A feeling of slight discomfort can actually help concentration. Your hands can either be loosely folded in your lap or gently cupped to receive the offering of peace and energy that will come your way. In the classic *The Tibetan Way of Living and Dying* Sogyal Rinpoche says:

> Sit as if you were a mountain, with all the unshakable, steadfast majesty of a mountain. ... The most essential part of this posture is to keep the back straight. ... The inner energy or prana will then flow easily through the subtle channels of the body, and your mind will find its true state of rest.

There are many different techniques for the next step, from reciting a mantra to focusing on the sound of your own breathing. According to Sogyal Rinpoche, 'The Buddha taught 84,000 different ways to tame and pacify the negative emotions.' However, I don't propose to go that far here. If you choose to meditate regularly each day, I suggest the breathing method. To do this, sit in a relaxed but alert position with your legs either crossed or straight out in front of you. Breathe naturally, and then listen to your breathing, concentrating particularly on the outward breath. When, after five or ten minutes, your breathing becomes almost too shallow to hear, extend your concentration to an awareness of the sounds of the world around you. For me, concentrating on external sounds comes easily. It might be the calls of the birds as they wake to the dawn, tree branches tap-tapping on the cottage roof, or the dogs snoring in the next room. And then there is the sound of the wind itself, or the noise of the crickets gearing up for another busy day. The more I listen, the more I realize that the sound of silence is very much alive, and that that 'silence' is no quieter than a five-piece jazz band.

As a further aid to concentration, some methods of meditation incorporate the recitation of a mantra. Definitions of a mantra vary, but in many cases it is a positive affirmation. Combined with breathing, it becomes a particularly powerful force for the concentration of energy.

One mantra that I find particularly powerful in my own life is one of 'breathing out love,' which is used in a form of transformational meditation. The full mantra goes like this: *'Breathe in the negativity ... turn it into love in the heart chakra ... and breathe out love.'* Say the words in your mind as you breathe.

To put the mantra into practice: take a slow, deep inward breath, simultaneously telling yourself to 'breathe in the negativity...' (whatever the particular situation or personality it is that you find disturbing). Next, on the 'turn' of the breath as it were, just before you breathe out, repeat to yourself, 'Turn it into love in the heart chakra. ...' Then, as you breathe out, say to yourself, '...and breathe out love.'

It is essential that you breathe as deeply as possible, and really feel the breath in the region of your heart chakra, which lies between and just a little below the breasts.

I find I use this meditation exercise to 'top off' my everyday meditation, and to align energy forces when things in my life start to go awry. I don't necessarily sit, but do it when I'm walking the dogs, waiting for a bus, or whenever I feel at all disturbed about something. My sister offered this gift to me; her friend gave it to her. That's the way the consciousness works. The act of channeling your energy to pour out love works in a truly miraculous way on the world about you.

Whatever method of meditation you choose in order to focus your concentration, the important—the essential— thing is to deal positively with any thoughts that intrude. One of the major problems people say they face when they start meditating is how to 'stop the thoughts.' Meditation is not contemplation. While contemplation has its place, you should be clear about the difference to get the most value out of the meditation exercise. This is 'time out' for your busy mind.

However, stilling that busy mind is not always easy, particularly at first. Some schools of meditation suggest that you deal with intrusive thoughts by pushing them away, gently but consistently and conscientiously, returning each time to the pinpoint of your concentration, whether this be an awareness of your breathing, reciting a mantra or listening to external sounds. Another way of achieving quietness is to concentrate on the gap between the thoughts. With time, you will find that the gap gets wider and wider, and that suddenly you are meditating.

Sogyal Rinpoche likens the thoughts and emotions to the waves and the ocean. He also says:

> When people begin to meditate, they often say that their thoughts are running riot, and have become wilder than ever before. But I reassure them and say that this is a good sign. Far from meaning that your thoughts have become wilder, it shows that you have become quieter, and you are finally aware of just how noisy your thoughts have always been. Don't be disheartened or give up. Whatever arises, just keep being present, keep returning to the breath, even in the midst of all the confusion. ...

Thoughts and emotions arise out of our minds just as the waves arise out of the sea. They are a necessary part of the sea's very essence, but at the same time they disturb the serenity of the water, and something akin to confusion results.

It is this confusion that we are trying to overcome. We are trying to banish the thoughts that beat up a storm in our minds. But the message from the great masters is that we can't simply sit down to meditate and quell a lifetime's lack of mental discipline by this action alone. Replacing the confusion with quiet is more a question of practice than willpower. I found that it pays to get into the habit of a regular meditation time and place. Setting up the habit is more important than trying to get rid of the thoughts. If you persevere in developing the habit, the skill will take care of itself.

Some masters advocate keeping your eyes open during meditation; others carry out the practice with the eyes closed; and there are others who meditate with their eyes focused downward on a single object. Personally, I find it easier to concentrate with my eyes closed, but this is a matter of individual preference.

Whatever method you choose, come out of the meditation slowly if you can—sometimes the phone rings in the middle of mine!—and then go about the chores of the day refreshed and much better able to cope. If you are interrupted halfway through and the meditation has been a fairly deep one, some practitioners recommend that you wash your hands with water, a cleansing ritual that symbolizes your return to the everyday world.

CENTERING

Although centering could be described as just another form of meditation, it differs from the meditations we have discussed above in its method. In the meditations I have described, you concentrate on being still; in centering, you 'travel' to the center of your being. Centering requires you to undertake a set of specific steps to help clear your mind of thoughts and emotions. This enables your core, or innermost being, to become receptive to the energies and forces inspired by your sixth sense or intuition.

Motivational teacher Alexander Everett is an expert in mental discipline who travels the world, passing on his knowledge and special brand of spiritualism. He claims the credit for pioneering the technique of centering. During one of his seminars

I was taught a number of methods for reaching this 'center.' The one that most appeals to me involves going deeper and deeper into yourself via the colors of the rainbow.

In this process of centering, you identify each color of the rainbow with an object: red might be a rose, orange the color of a sunset, yellow the flowers that grow amid the scrub on a beachy headland, and so on. Having allocated a symbol for each color, take half a minute or so to visualize each symbol right through to the color violet at the end of the rainbow. The idea is that once you have progressed through each color, you will have arrived at the spiritual center of your being. This is the place where your intuition is most active. This is where you are connected to your soul or the subconscious part of you, and where you can communicate with the forces in and around you. And this is where you will find a quality of peace you never knew existed.

Stay at your center, keeping your mind blank for as long as possible between thoughts, for about fifteen minutes. Be alert to the colors and images that are thrown up on the screen of your mind. At first, there may be nothing, a non-color, not even black. Then you may find that different colors beam and fade, or see shapes or faces or unidentifiable images that wriggle around on the screen like a family of amoebas. Just sit quietly. Make no judgment. Don't try to question or to work things out. Merely observe. You will sense intuitively when the fifteen minutes are up and it is time to return. Come back to base gradually, traveling backwards through the spectrum of the rainbow from violet to red.

I have added my own rider, as it were, to Everett's technique, which you may find useful. It happened that, after a spate of attitudinal counseling, I set out to find the little girl within myself. The child within us is often sacrificed to the seriousness of life. It is often lost, and sometimes never known. The child is the playful me, the less-worried me, the more mischievous me. I now visit my 'little girl' each day where she lives in the violet center at the end of the rainbow, but I treat both her and myself by bringing her back up the rainbow with me, and we both enjoy the experience. Inevitably, I get caught up in the day's experiences, and she tends to slide back down again, but the habit of bringing her home each morning is a good one, and I keep her with me each day for as long as she is comfortable. If finding the happy, playful side of your nature appeals to you, you too can try this technique. Although giving vent to the playful side of our nature is fun, it is also a bit sad that this aspect of us got lost in the first place.

Unfortunately, to the best of my knowledge, you cannot bone up on the rainbow technique by reading a book, because Alexander Everett hasn't written one. Meanwhile, if you need a more detailed description of centering, one of Alexander Everett's pupils, Jess Stearn, has written a book, *The Power of Alpha Thinking,* that describes a similar process. One of the methods he advocates is that of walking down a flight of stairs to get to the intuitive center of your being, remembering, of course, to walk back up again afterwards. While there are many ways to access your center, I find Alexander Everett's rainbow method works best for me.

POSITIVE THINKING

Many books are written about positive thinking and taking control of your life, and there are many counselors and teachers of attitudinal thinking. Life-long attitudes are hard to change merely by reading a book; on the other hand, continued counseling as we cope with change, change, change, is expensive and is not necessarily the way to go either. I advocate a mix of both. If you have the time and money, shop around a bit for a qualified and well-regarded counselor or teacher to help you delve into the background of why you are as you are and try to get some sort of picture of the real inner you.

Of all the books I have read on positive thinking, Norman Vincent Peale's *You Can If You Think You Can* probably helped me most, although it was written many years ago. It is often a question of the right book at the right time.

REIKI

This is another method of channeling the universal energy for the general good of all. The word 'Reiki' comes from a Japanese word that refers to the universal life-force or energy that exists within and around all of us. Reiki is a method of hands-on healing where the practitioner is a conduit for focusing this universal energy to work on the mind and body of those in need. Although the technique of using energy for healing goes back to antiquity, in the latter part of the last century it was rediscovered by the dean of a Christian seminary in Japan, Dr. Mikao Usui. Dr. Usui had been challenged by his students to show how Jesus performed his miracles, and in his quest to uncover the ancient knowledge, he studied different religions and languages and traveled to many countries.

Today Reiki is being practiced by more and more people all over the world. Anyone can learn Reiki and experience the rewards of using it on themselves, their families and their friends.

I have found that responses to a Reiki treatment vary with the individual. People on whom I have used the technique have reacted in different ways. Some feel so relaxed they have the desire to fall straight into bed, while for others the effect is less obvious. On the occasions I have received a Reiki treatment myself, I am left with a feeling of relaxation so total that I find it almost impossible to get off the massage couch. Following this, my body seems to pulsate with energy.

Reiki is taught by a Reiki master, and before you can practice it yourself you need to be initiated or 'fine-tuned' to the universal energy waves. Reiki initiates are often invited to take part in a Reiki crisis line. This is a network that sends a healing energy to a request for help. If someone is ill or in trouble, the call goes out for each volunteer to spend five minutes of the meditative part of his or her day sending Reiki healing to that person. Each person calls the next person on the list, and it is quite amazing to experience the sense of connectedness you get from that tiny amount of effort from people who are, in most cases, total strangers. What you put into life, you certainly get back—many, many times over.

Reiki can work for animals too. One of the funniest stories told at a session I attended was that of Chookie, the chicken who thinks she is human. Chookie responded so well to a session of Reiki that she continues to follow her owners around demanding further treatment. I have used

Reiki to treat my dogs for small wounds that have begun to fester, ulcers in the eye and sore ears, all of which have healed without visits to the vet and expensive antibiotics.

YOGA

This is another technique for freeing up and using the universal energy. Yoga was first developed and practiced in India in ancient times, and one of its main aims is to increase the supply of energy to the body. It is a great way to discipline both mind and body for overall fitness.

Paul Galbraith, in his excellent book *Reversing Ageing*, says that among the benefits that will accrue from the practice of yoga are those of gaining extra energy, looking and feeling younger, and living longer, as well as achieving more positive mental and emotional states.

To start a course on yoga, ask around or check your local paper. There's sure to be a center near you, and this technique is probably better taught than gleaned from a book or a magazine, since it is all too easy to pull muscles and ligaments at the beginning.

There are many other methods of getting in touch with yourself and with others, of improving your attitude, of ridding both mind and body of the poisons that have accumulated over time. Once you've got the basics, incorporating a form of quieting your mind and body into your daily life is really up to you. There are just two things to be aware of. First, as I have said, make sure that your instructor is qualified; and, second, take care not to become a 'spiritual junkie' or someone who bounces from course to course, sampling everything and anything that is offered and mastering little.

Chapter Twelve

Acknowledging the Godforce

All places that the eye of heaven visits
Are to a wise man ports and happy havens.

—*William Shakespeare*

The processes I have outlined so far lead ultimately to that special brand of peace at the eye of the cyclone that we've had in mind all the way through. To arrive at the center is to acknowledge your own spirituality, to know without doubt that you are not alone, that the godforce will not desert you when you most need it.

But what is the godforce? Who or what is God?

In a letter dated May 23, 1955, Jung wrote: 'For me, God is a mystery that cannot be unveiled, and to which I must attribute only one quality: that it exists.' For as many people who believe in the existence of God, there are as many who don't. As any first-year philosophy student who has waded through the reams of lengthy papers that attempt to prove and disprove the existence of God will attest, the greatest minds in the world endlessly debate the point. At the same time, it is interesting to note that most of us acknowledge the existence of a prime mover, a force or an energy or some form of power that keeps the universe ticking like a well-maintained clock. If you change what is, after all, only a label, all of a sudden there are millions more believers.

The Christians believe in Christ; the Muslims worship Allah; the Buddhists kneel at the feet of the Buddha; the supporters of Krishna Consciousness humble themselves before the Supreme Personality of Godhead. In other words, all those who believe that a greater force exists than that of the individual have a belief in an external source of energy, although they may not call it God.

Yogis, human-potential teachers and other individuals arrive at their knowledge of God in other ways. Rebel Catholic priest Matthew Fox believes in God, but is wary of the way in which humans promote God. He says, 'Religion should be a way of life, not an institutional thing. And prayer is about the body, not the head. It's about awakening the courage in our souls.'

Preeminent scholar and teacher of mythology Joseph Campbell believed in the existence of what he called an 'impersonal god, namely a transcendent ground or energy in itself.'

For author and lecturer Stuart Wilde we are part of 'the Force,' and the Force is the spiritual energy that shapes our lives. The Force is God and, therefore, we are God. He says:

> As you develop yourself spiritually, people will come to you, for the Force knows how to make use of its supporters, and it will allow you, through the intrinsic value of your spiritual energy, to go further, to shine even more brightly. And you will understand more and more deeply that what you are is God. There is nothing you cannot do. There are no real limits to your capacity.

With awareness and balance and, most of all, love, you can reach the center.

Alexander Everett offers the same message in a slightly different way. He teaches oneness; that all living things are part of one another, joined by our spirituality, or soul, to the power at the center of the universe.

Following my husband's death, a dear friend of mine—a committed Catholic who has certainly had her fair share of troubles—called long-distance from South Africa.

'Accept,' she said. 'You simply must *accept* what has happened.' There was an urgency in her tone that, to this day, impresses me as much as her actual words.

But I was coming from a long way back, and it took me some time to accept, to admit, that there was a greater force than me. I could see the manifestation of a controller all around me in the changing seasons, in the cyclical nature of plant life, but I was unable to apply it to myself and my own set of circumstances.

It was, finally, by traveling the path I have outlined in this book that I found resolution. It became clear that if I wanted to reach the peace at the center, my most sensible course was to align myself with the energy that emanates from that center. I came gradually to see that this energy could be called by any other name—be it nature, the universe, the Force or God.

For me, all paths now lead towards the center. I am letting go of the old, tired conditioning, the doubts and worries, the fears and the panic that in today's parapsychological jargon are called 'baggage.' I have embarked on a journey that I am confident will enable me increasingly to *accept* the challenges and disappointments of life just as I have no problem accepting and celebrating the successes and the joys. I am learning to see life as one side of the coin, death as the other; joy on one side, sorrow on the other. And I have been fortunate in that my own experiences have promoted within me something more than faith: the humility of *knowing* that there is a God.

For me, the godforce is love, nothing more complicated than that. And belief in a godforce encompasses love of our planet, of animals, of our fellow human beings and, most importantly, love and acceptance of ourselves. Where there is love, there cannot be fear or desperation. There simply is no room. If the fear or panic rises up, it is surprising how the three simple words 'God help me' banish the gloom.

We are all in this together, this great life adventure, voyaging in a giant ark to a destination unknown. Our solidarity, our oneness with each other and all living things, is our strength. We can reach out and touch each other, and know that we are not alone. In my writing of this book and your reading of it, this is something we have achieved between us.

There is a great comfort, and a still greater joy, in that.

Resources

....

ORGANIZATIONS AND SELF-HELP GROUPS

ACCORD
   1941 Bishop's Lane, Ste. 202
   Louisville, KY 40218
   (800) 346-3087

American Association of Retired Persons
   Widowed Persons Services
   601 E St., N.W.
   Washington, DC 20049
   (202) 434-2277

Association for Death Education and Counseling
   638 Prospect Ave.
   Hartford, CT 06105-4298
   (203) 586-7503

Bereavement and Loss Center of New York
   170 E. 83rd St.
   New York, NY 10028
   (212) 879-5655

Center for New Directions
   P. O. Box 1609
   Columbus, OH 43216-1609
   (614) 227-5333

Centering Corporation
   1531 N. Saddle Creek Rd.
   Omaha, NE 68104
   (402) 553-1200

The Compassionate Friends
P. O. Box 3696
Oak Brook, IL 60522-3696
(708) 990-0010

Grief Education Institute
6795 E. Tennessee Ave., Ste. 425
Denver, CO 80224
(303) 758-6048

National Self-Help Clearing House
25 W. 43rd St., Rm. 620
New York, NY 10036
(212) 642-2944

Parents Without Partners
National Helpline
(800) 637-7974

THEOS (They Help Each Other Spiritually) Foundation
322 Blvd. of the Allies, Ste. 105
Pittsburgh, PA 15222
(412) 471-7779

Widowed Information and Consultation Services
15417 First Ave. South
Seattle, WA 98148
(206) 246-6142

or

223 N. Yakima Ave.
Tacoma, WA 98403
(206) 272-8092

Widowed Persons Association of California
P. O. Box 60619
Sacramento, CA 95860-0619
(916) 972-9443

PROFESSIONAL THERAPY AND COUNSELING

American Association of Marriage and Family Therapy
    1133 15th St., N.W., Ste. 300
    Washington, DC 20005
    Send stamped self-addressed envelope

American Psychiatric Association
    1400 K St., N.W.
    Washington, DC 20005
    (202) 682-6000

American Psychoanalytic Association
    309 E. 49th St.
    New York, NY 10017
    (212) 752-0450

American Psychological Association
    750 First St., N.E.
    Washington, DC 20002
    (202) 336-5500

International Association for Analytical Psychology
    Postfach 115
    8042
    Zurich, Switzerland

U.S. centers for the study of analytic psychology include the C. G. Jung Educational Center of Houston, (713) 524-8253; the C. G. Jung Institute of San Francisco, (415) 771-8055; the C. G. Jung Institute of Chicago, (312) 475-4848; and the C. G. Jung Institute of New York, (212) 986-5458.

National Association for Mental Health
    1021 Prince St.
    Alexandria, VA 22314-2971
    (703) 684-7722

JOURNALS AND NEWSLETTERS

Bereavement: A Magazine of Hope and Healing
  8133 Telegraph Dr.
  Colorado Springs, CO 80920
  (719) 282-1948

Death and Life Newsletter
  Prof. David Meagher
  Brooklyn College Thanatology Program
  Department of Health Science
  Brooklyn, NY 11210
  (718) 951-5026 Ext. 5553

In Accord
  1941 Bishop's Lane, Ste. 202
  Louisville, KY 40218
  (800) 346-3087

Omega: The Journal of Death and Dying
  Baywood Publishing Co.
  26 Austin Ave.
  Amityville, NY 11701
  (516) 691-1270

Notes

....

PAGE 1:   Michel de Montaigne, 'To philosophize is to learn
            how to die,' from *The Essays of Michel de Montaigne*,
            trans. and ed. by M. A. Screech, Allen Lane, London,
            1991, p. 95. Montaigne was a French essayist who
            lived in the sixteenth century.

PAGE 4:   M. Scott Peck, *The Road Less Travelled*, Arrow,
            London, 1992, p. 15.

PAGE 5:   Australian Bureau of Statistics, Deaths Australia 1993,
            Information Services, Canberra, 1994, Catalogue
            3302.0, Table 8.

PAGE 9:   Pat Rodegast & Judith Stanton (eds), *Emmanuel's
            Book*, Bantam, New York, 1987, p. 170.

PAGE 12:   Harriet Klein, 'The future precedes the past: Time in
            Toba,' *Word*, vol. 38, p. 179.

PAGE 13:   Clifford Geertz, *The Interpretation of Cultures*,
            Hutchinson, London, 1975, pp. 389–98.

PAGE 17:   Rodegast & Stanton, *Emmanuel's Book*.

PAGE 19:   Stuart Wilde, *Life Wasn't Meant to Be a Struggle*,
            White Dove International Inc., Taos, NM, 1987.
            Darryl Reanney, *The Death of Forever*, Longman
            Cheshire, Melbourne, 1991.

PAGE 23:   Jack Kornfield & Paul Breiter (comp. & eds), *A Still
            Forest Pool: The Insight Meditation of Achaan Chah*,
            Theosophical Publishing House, Wheaton, IL, 1991,
            p. 73.

PAGE 25:   Kahlil Gibran, *The Prophet*, Heinemann, London,
            1970, p. 19.

PAGE 33: Rodegast & Stanton, *Emmanuel's Book*, p. 127.

PAGE 41: *Bhagavad Gita*, trans. Juan Mascaro, Penguin, Harmondsworth, 1962, p. 113.

PAGES 44–5: Clarissa Pinkola Estés, *Women Who Run with the Wolves*, Ballantine, New York, 1992.

PAGE 45: Richard Bach, *The Bridge Across Forever*, Dell, New York, 1986; *Illusions*, Dell, New York, 1989.
James Redfield, *The Celestine Prophecy*, Warner, New York, 1994.
Ben Okri, *The Famished Road*, Vintage, London, 1992.

PAGE 49: Siegfried Sassoon, 'Microcosmos,' *Collected Poems by Siegfried Sassoon*, Faber & Faber, London, 1947, p. v.

PAGE 55: Gibran, *The Prophet*, p. 20.

PAGES 63–64: Portia Nelson, 'Autobiography in Five Short Chapters,' in *There's a Hole in My Sidewalk*, Popular Library, New York, 1977.

PAGE 68: Stuart Wilde, *The Force*, White Dove International Inc., Taos, NM, 1987, pp. 65 and 67.

PAGE 71: Wayne Dyer, *You'll See It When You Believe It*, Avon, New York, 1990.

PAGE 73: Julian Boul Noies, *And the Walls Came Tumbling Down*, Spectrum, Melbourne, 1983, p. 73.
Reinhold Niebuhr, 'The Serenity Prayer.'

PAGE 83: Gibran, *The Prophet*, p. 93.

PAGES 85: Aniela Jaffe (ed.), *C. G. Jung: Word and Image*, Princeton University Press, Princeton, NJ, 1979, p. 228.

PAGE 86: Henry Reed, *Edgar Cayce on Channeling Your Higher Self*, Association for Research and Enlightenment Inc., Warner Books, New York, p. 45.

PAGE 87: Sigmund Freud, *The Interpretation of Dreams*, Penguin, Harmondsworth, England 1976, p. 107.

PAGE 89:   Jaffe, *C. G. Jung*, p. 213.

PAGE 91:   Thelma Thompson, quoting her father, in Dale
                Carnegie, *How to Stop Worrying and Start Living*,
                Chaucer Press, Suffolk, p. 178.

PAGE 99:   John Milton, *Paradise Lost*, Methuen, London, 1926,
                i. 254–55.
                Sogyal Rinpoche, *The Tibetan Way of Living and
                Dying*, Rider, London, 1992, p. 46.

PAGES 104:   Sogyal Rinpoche, *The Tibetan Way of Living and
                Dying*, p. 65.

PAGE 105:   Sogyal Rinpoche, *The Tibetan Way of Living and
                Dying*, p. 68.

PAGE 107:   Sogyal Rinpoche, *The Tibetan Way of Living and
                Dying*, p. 73.

PAGE 110:   Jess Stearn, *The Power of Alpha Thinking*, NAL
                Dutton, New York, 1989.

PAGE 113:   Paul Galbraith, *Reversing Ageing*, Lothian, Pt.
                Melbourne, Australia 1993.

PAGE 115:   William Shakespeare, *Richard II*, I. iii. 274.

PAGE 117:   Jaffe, *C. G. Jung*, p. 209.

PAGE 118:   Matthew Fox, lecture notes, University of Western
                Australia.

PAGE 118:   Betty Sue Flowers (ed.), *The Power of Myth*,
                Doubleday, London, 1989, p. 213, Joseph
                Campbell, interviewed by Bill Moyers.

PAGE 118:   Wilde, *The Force*, p. 74.

PAGE 119:   Alexander Everett, P. O. Box 456, Veneta, OR, USA
                97487.

Further Reading

As a trip to your local bookstore will highlight, there are many books available on the topics covered in this book. Listed below are a few of my personal favorites.

UNDERSTANDING DEATH

Gibran, K. *The Prophet.* New York: Knopf, 1995.

Kubler-Ross, E. *On Death and Dying.* New York: Collier, 1993.

Kushner, H. S. *When Bad Things Happen to Good People.* New York: Avon, 1981.

Reanney, D. *Living Forever.* Morrow, 1995.

Reanney, D. *Music of the Mind.* Seven Hills Books, 1994.

Rodegast, P., and Stanton, J. *Emmanuel's Book.* New York: Bantam, 1987.

CHILDREN AND GRIEVING

Grollman, E. A. *Talking About Death: A Dialogue Between Parent and Child.* Boston: Beacon, 1990.

Olson, B. K. *Energy Secrets for Tired Mothers on the Run.* Deerfield Beach, FL: Health Communications Inc., 1993.

Youngs, B. B. *Helping Your Teenager Deal with Stress.* Los Angeles: Tarcher, 1986.

DREAMING

Garfield, P. *Creative Dreaming.* New York: Ballantine Books, 1990.

Garfield, P. *Women's Bodies, Women's Dreams.* New York: Ballantine Books, 1991.

Jung, C. G. *Man and His Symbols.* New York: Dell/Laurel, 1968.

THE PRACTICAL SIDE OF CARRYING ON

Morgan, E. *Dealing Creatively with Death: A Manual of Death Education and Simple Burial.* Barclay House, 1990.

Clifford, D. *Nolo's Simple Will Book.* Berkeley, CA: Nolo Press, 1986.

COPING WITH SEXUALITY

Winks, C., and Semans, A. *The Good Vibrations Guide to Sex.* Pittsburgh: Cleis Press, 1994.

QUIETING YOUR MIND AND BODY

Baginski, B. J., and Sharamon, S. *Reiki: Universal Life Energy.* Mendocino, CA: Life Rhythm Publications, 1988.

Covey, S. *The Seven Habits of Highly Effective People.* New York: Fireside, 1990.

Dyer, W. *Real Magic.* New York: HarperCollins, 1993.

Estés, C. P. *Women Who Run with the Wolves,* New York: Ballantine, 1992.

Galbraith, P. *Reversing Ageing.* Pt. Melbourne: Lothian, 1993.

Gawler, I. *You Can Conquer Cancer.* Seven Hills Books, 1994.

Horan, P. *Empowerment Through Reiki.* Wilmot, WI: Lotus Light Publications, 1992.

Meares, A. *The Wealth Within.* Seven Hills Books, 1994.

Peale, N. V. *You Can If You Think You Can.* New York: Simon & Schuster, 1988.

Stearn, J. *The Power of Alpha Thinking.* New York: NAL Dutton, 1989.

Stein, D. *Essential Reiki.* Freedom, CA: The Crossing Press, 1995.

Whitfield, C. *Healing the Child Within.* Orlando, FL: Health Communications, 1987.

THE GODFORCE

Campbell, J. *The Power of Myth.* New York: Doubleday, 1991.

Peck, M. Scott. *The Road Less Travelled.* New York: Touchstone, 1988.

Sogyal Rinpoche. *The Tibetan Way of Living and Dying.* New York: Harper, 1992.

Wilde, S. *The Force.* Taos, NM: White Dove, 1987.

Index

action 66–70
   see also activities, attitude; change;
     exercise; friendship; play
     group; positive thinking
activities 28, 35–39, 70–71
age pensioners *see* funeral
anger 67
   see also attitude
attitude 36, 46, 66–67, 69–70, 72,
     96, 111, 114, 119–20
   of other people 93–96
   towards death 1, 5, 16, 20–21, 94,
     119–20
   see also centering; languages and
     cultures; meditation; positive
     thinking; Reiki

Bach, Richard 45
balance 68, 103, 119
bank accounts *see* death
belief patterns 36, 72
   see also attitude; languages and
     cultures; religion
Buddhism 13–14, 21, 23, 118

Campbell, Joseph 118
Cayce, Edgar 19, 44, 86
centering 102, 108–10
   see also Everett, Alexander
change 40, 51
   moving 79–80
   see also activities; children;
     sexuality
children:
   behavioral changes 57–60
   mother's leaning, dangers of
     58–60
   play group 61–62

professional advice 60
   their grief 57
Christianity 19, 45, 118
crying 26–31, 67, 94
cultures *see* languages and cultures

death:
   bank accounts 78–79
   cyclical nature of life and death
     11, 15–16, 21, 58, 119
   death certificate 78
   estate 78
   financial problems 51
   legal expenses 79
   reactions of other people 93–96
   taboos 4, 11, 14, 20, 58, 75, 94
   see also attitude; change; children;
     funeral; grieving; life after
     death; psychotherapy; will
Department of Veterans' Affairs 78
dreams 43, 85–89
   dream school 86–87
   recording 46, 87–88
   remembering 87–88
   symbols 87–89
   unconscious, link with 85–86
Dyer, Wayne 71

Emerson, Ralph Waldo 19
Emmanuel's Book 9, 17–18, 33
estate *see* death
Estés, Clarissa Pinkola 44
Everett, Alexander 108–10, 119
   see also centering
executor *see* will
exercise 28, 35–36, 38–39

The Herbal Menopause Book: *Herbs, Nutrition, and Other Natural Therapies*

By Amanda Mcquade Crawford, M.N.I.M.H.

A comprehensive volume providing a wealth of natural self-care therapies including herbal formulas, nutrition, vitamin supplements, exercise, massage, and visualizations for women facing the health issues that arise in premenopause, menopause, and postmenopause.

$16.95 · Paper · 0-89594-799-4

The Natural Remedy Book for Women

By Diane Stein

This best-seller includes information on ten natural healing methods—vitamins and minerals, herbs, naturopathy, homeopathy and cell salts, amino acids, acupressure, aromatherapy, flower essences, gemstones and emotional healing. Remedies from all ten methods are given for fifty common health problems.

$16.95 · Paper · 0-89594-525-8

Please look for these books
at your local bookstore or order from
The Crossing Press
P.O. Box 1048, Freedom, CA 95019.

Add $2.50 for the first book and 50¢ for each
additional book. Or call toll free 800-777-1048
with your credit card order.